CALL SIGNS

Stories from the little known
US Army airplane community

STEVE KOENIG

CONTENTS

Call Signs is a collection of true short stories as provided by the pilots of the Army's little known, underappreciated airplane community. These stories are of the Cold War and shooting war pilots who did what was asked and lived to tell about. Some of these stories are boring, some will make you laugh and some will even seem unbelievable, but as truth is stranger than fiction, these stories really happened. This book is dedicated to all Army Fixed Wing pilots who continue to do the mission with the motto: "Alone, Unarmed and Unafraid."

ARMY 427

After my transition to Army fixed-wing, I was assigned as a junior pilot at Fort Sill Oklahoma in late 1977. As a junior pilot in the flight detachment, I got to fly the smaller aircraft of the fleet to build my flight time and fixed wing experience. I started in the T42A Cochise, the U8 G and F, and the U-21, an unpressurized version of a Beech King Air 90. They were comfortable in flight and very rugged, but not altogether mechanically reliable. Being a good Soldier, I kept my head down, did my job and built up my flight time. Life as a fixed wing pilot was so much nicer than flying helicopters and I was enjoying the opportunity.

For whatever reason, my commander noticed my dedication and hard work so assigned me a flight to make any male pilot jealous. I was assigned to fly a U8 to Oklahoma City to pick up the gorgeous, blond and beautiful Miss Oklahoma 1978, Ms Kendi Brown. Ms Brown was making a statewide tour of military bases known as morale, welfare and recreation visits. I was going to be her personal pilot for her visit to Fort Sill. And as they say, women love a man in uniform, especially pilots!

CW2 Randall and U-8 (Army 427)

I was assigned Army 427, a well-equipped VIP U-8 for the relatively short flight to Oklahoma City to pick up Ms Brown and deliver her in style down to the Fort. The plan was for her to be met at the Army Airfield by the Post Commander, his entourage and of course my boss, the Flight Detachment Commander.

I was the flying pilot for the trip and the flight up was uneventful. Weather was as predicted with low ceilings and some haze and fog forecast. We parked at the Oklahoma City airport Fixed Base Operation (FBO) and got out to meet our beautiful passenger.

Miss Oklahoma 1978, Ms Kendi Brown

After introductions in the FBO, we gave her a standard passenger briefing, introduced her to her escort, a Captain from the post and told her about the flight and weather. Then we helped her and her escort officer get buckled in. Because of her title and duties, she seemed relaxed and comfortable getting in our aircraft. With little fanfare, we departed for Ft Sill.

After take-off we flew in the clouds for most the flight. It was reasonably smooth but flying without any reference to the ground or world around you is somewhat of an eerie sensation. But the more you fly on instruments, the more confident and easier it is. In fact, I enjoy flying without any reference to the outside world. To me, flying without seeing is the epitome of pilot skill, something that had been pioneered by General Jimmy Doolittle in the 1930's, and requires a lot of common sense.

The weather was as forecast coming back to Ft Sill so we knew that we would be flying a Precision Approach Radar (PAR) procedure to minimums. A PAR was state of the art in 1978 for military aircraft. From around two thousand feet above the ground, a radar controller tells you when to descend, what heading to fly and for the most part, talks you to the ground or until you break out of the clouds and can see the ground. New technology has made the PAR almost obsolete, but the military still uses the system to this day.

We checked in with the Ft Sill control tower and were given a weather update of fog and two hundred foot ceilings. So, as I was in the left seat flying the PAR approach to minimums, I called for the landing gear down as we began our descent. Even though I was concentrating on the PAR, I was surprised to hear and feel a very loud clunk. The plane yawed significantly and the light in the landing gear handle changed to red; meaning it was not safe to land. Following standard procedures, I asked the other pilot to bring the gear up and then down again, or in aviation speak, cycle the gear. He did as requested, but to the same effect: red light in the gear handle and an unsafe gear situation.

I flew down to 200 feet above the ground and broke out of the fog. Despite it being such a miserable day, I decided to make a low 'fly-by' for the control tower to confirm or deny my dilemma. "Your left wheel is not down. The nose and right wheels seem to be down and locked, but you don't appear to have a left wheel." came the answer from the tower. In the cockpit everything possible was tried to resolve the problem, from pumping the offending gear down with a hand operated emergency pump, to 'yawing' the plane to use the force of the wind to get the gear to lock down; but to no avail. There was nothing left to do but prepare for a landing on two wheels. Of course, circling the airfield at such low level had our passenger's attention too so when we were certain this would not be a normal landing, we told her what had happened and how to brace for the landing. Miss Oklahoma was very calm and sensible throughout. Destined now to arrive in some sort of crash landing, I circled the airfield at two hundred feet until emergency equipment could be brought out. The Medivac helicopter responded to our Mayday call and positioned itself alongside the fire trucks halfway down the runway.

When I was completely ready, I brought the plane around and landed on the right wheel, then the nose wheel; sinking lowly onto the left wing and sliding gracefully to a halt on the center line of the runway. Emergency rescue crews sped into action as a small fire broke out under the left wing and Miss Oklahoma and her army captain escort, followed by myself and my co-pilot, evacuated the plane. And although I was hoping to give her a good impression in my uniform and flying skills, I know that this wasn't the way I had hoped to impress her. Not exactly the reception we had planned for Ms. Brown, but we were safe and uninjured. In true pageant fashion, she thanked all the response teams, hoped in the waiting car and departed for her event on post. We flew her back to Norman, OK later that day in a different aircraft.

The post-crash investigation revealed that when I had put the landing gear handle down, an actuator which operated the left wheel had shattered, so it would not go down. The U-8F and I had a long discussion after this one. Thankfully, the only damage to the aircraft was to the flaps and left aileron. And, because of the high profile passenger, all the witnesses on the airfield, poor weather and safely landing the aircraft with minimal damage, I was awarded the Army Broken Wing Award. The Army level award is presented to Army pilots who "display extraordinary skill, judgment and technique during an in-flight emergency. In spite of extreme circumstances which might have lead to catastrophic results, a successful landing was achieved through application of the highest degree of proficiency and discretion."

Army 427 On the runway (US Army photo)

I might not have gotten the girl, but she still had the poise to leave me a memento, a personalized thank you note.

Kendi Brown
Miss Oklahoma 1978

"HOURS AND HOURS OF BOREDOM..."

The Army has a history of art and cartoons documenting the stories of the Soldiers around the world. This holds true for the airplane community as well. One of the most famous airplane cartoonists is CW4 (retired) Bob Snead.

Although maintenance problems, bad weather and other unusual activities are no laughing matter, when you survive something you weren't expecting there's always a wave of relief. During his career, CW4 (retired) Bob Snead took his flying experiences and captured them in his cartoons. Originally published in *"Hours and Hours of Boredom..."* published by El Paso Graphics Group, in 1983, Bob has given permission for his cartoons to be incorporated into "Call Signs".

"...SHOPPING JUNKET... THEY WENT BACK TO THE HOTEL TO GET THEIR PERSONAL BAGGAGE..."

ARMY 089

Flying around weather and dodging a few storms is something that every pilot has had to do from time to time. So, when we were assigned to pick up a three-star general, the Army G-1, Army Personnel Director, on April 10th, 1979 at Dallas and fly him to Ft. Sill in Lawton, Oklahoma, it seemed like it would be one of those days.

I and another pilot were assigned a VIP U-8, tail number 76089, so our callsign for that flight would be "Army 089". The U8 was designed for transporting small groups of VIPS. A modified Beechcraft Bonanza, with a larger cabin at the request of the US Army, it has the same wings and tail as a Bonanza but carries up to ten people in the longer, wider and higher cabin. With the shape and size of the airplane, Beechcraft christened it the "Queen Air". Besides the room for the VIPs, the aircraft was certified for instrument flight and equipped with weather radar. Our flight briefing indicated that there would be storms in the afternoon but given our timeframe, they were not expected to be a problem.

CW2 Randall and U-8 "Army 089" taken prior to April 10th flight

When preflighting the plane, we noticed that the weather radar wasn't working, but that wasn't unusual in the U-8. We flew to Dallas without incident and awaited the general. We did see a line of thunderstorms but they seemed pretty far west. If the general arrived on time, all would be okay, but with Spring weather, you could just never tell.

U-8 cockpit with large weather radar

The G-1 wasn't too late so we seated him and departed for Fort Sill flying at 10,000 feet just above the cloud tops. The first 15 minutes weren't bad but growing storms now appeared between us and Ft. Sill. The storms were so tall that in order to see the tops I had to lean far forward in my seat and look straight up through the top of the windscreen. I kept thinking: "Boy, I wish that weather radar was working." The storm clouds overhanging our flight path were huge and unnerving. They were well above the operating altitude of the U-8. We were going to have to fly through them to get to Ft. Sill. The Henry Post Army Airfield control tower at Fort Sill reported that the storms had not yet reached the airport so we began a let-down into the "clag" (aviators' slang for pea-soup clouds). We were also flying directly underneath the anvil of the thunderstorm, but only experienced light turbulence. So far, so good I thought.

We planned our approach and began our descending through the clouds about 10 miles from the field. We were starting to feel like weather wasn't that bad and that the flight was going to work out okay when quite unexpectedly everything went wrong. Without warning, hail stones the size of tennis balls pounded the airplane. It looked to me like we were flying into a vast sea of white Styrofoam cups hitting us at 160 knots and the sound it made pounding the delicate outer skin of the plane was indescribable. We could not hear anything because of the noise, and I instinctively ducked down below the glare-shield because it seemed the windscreen might implode at any moment. As the hailstones hurled themselves towards us, the turbulence began to increase, very slowly and ominously.

I glanced out my side window and to my horror, I watched huge pieces of the wing rubber deice boot tear off and fly away while leaving bits of rubber flapping wildly in the slipstream. I was not sure how we were managing to stay airborne; we were staggering around like a drunken sailor. Then, without any fanfare, the hailstorm stopped as quickly as it started, and it was blissfully quiet. We were still in the clouds, but we could hear again and more importantly talk with air traffic control.

But the peace and quiet was short lived. It started to get very dark in the cockpit; an unworldly deep green, followed by a sudden and violent entry into unimaginably heavy rain and extreme turbulence, the likes of which I had never imagined in my life, and of which I prayed I would survive and never experience again. The aircraft was out of control and both of us frantically tried to hold onto the yoke but severe up-and-down drafts physically jerked the yoke from our hands.

The noise was once again deafening. And, the sheer volume of the rain was also leaking into the cockpit through the seams around the windscreen, misting us and the cockpit in a fine spray. We were shouting at each other to hold the yolk, and together we struggled to try and keep the plane under control against the wild external forces. The torrent of rain was of an unbelievable volume and the turbulence was so violent it was hard for me to imagine how we would survive.

Even with everything going on, I heard a loud banging noise over the sounds of chaos the storm was making. I assumed I was hearing the plane breaking apart. But, when I turned my head to look, I saw the General's briefcase banging around inside the cabin, with him holding onto his armrests for dear life. For some odd reason, at that moment I thought: "I bet his speech doesn't go very well today....." And that thought made me chuckle a bit even as we were tossed about.

The aircraft had a mind of its own and suddenly we began an uncontrolled climb. The flying pilot pulled the power levers to 'idle' and pointed the nose down at steeper and steeper angles. The 'vertical' speed indicator was pegged at a maximum rate of climb of greater than

6000 feet per minute and no matter what we did with the controls the aircraft wallowed violently out of control. And if things weren't bad enough we heard the controller on the radio, matter-of-factly stating: "There is a confirmed tornado at your nine o'clock position on the ground five miles west of the airport. I see you are making a missed approach. We are abandoning the tower. Good luck."

The radios went silent. We weren't making a missed approach at all; we were totally out of control. The instrument panel vibrated so much in its spring mounted shock-resistant position that the gauges simply could not be read. All we could do was to keep the blue part of the aircraft attitude indicators pointed towards the top of the panel. The other gauges were useless. A bolt of lightning hit the plane with a blinding flash and huge crash and thunderous bang. The tornado on the ground had knocked out all of the navigation aids and all the radios had stopped working. We had no way of knowing where we were. I resigned myself to the fact that we wouldn't make it out of this violent storm; I was convinced the aircraft would break up in flight at any moment and fall to earth. With that picture in my mind a kind of peace settled over me as I stopped being afraid and began to cope to the best of my ability. I do recall thinking that my last visible image while alive would be the earth streaking upwards to greet our wingless fuselage. The violence of the turbulence was so severe, that it bruised my shoulders against the restraining straps.

We were in an uncontrolled climb from 1,500 feet above the ground to 11,000 feet, and somehow managed to turn the aircraft to the east, away from the storm. Within minutes of making this turn the rain stopped, the turbulence abated, and we flew back out into clear skies. What a change a few minutes could make. No more noise. No more turbulence. It was a bright sunny day, and death was no longer knocking. We could see the Dallas-Oklahoma City turnpike east of Ft

Sill and we simultaneously shouted that we should land on the freeway, because we were unsure how long the severely damaged plane would continue to fly. We flew back under the deck of the oncoming storm, outside the clouds this time.

We both saw the Lawton airport as we were descending towards the freeway so decided to land there instead. As we touched down on the runway, I saw the tornado on the ground about half a mile away at the north end of the airport. During our landing roll out at mid-field we watched in horror as the tornado destroyed the control tower and the fire station. We taxied off the runway as fast as we could and headed towards the commercial passenger ramp where a lone airliner sat unattended in relative quiet. The airport appeared to have been abandoned. We quickly shut down the engines, hustled the general out of the aircraft, and ran towards the passenger terminal with debris beginning to fall around us. Once inside the building, breathless and pretty much mentally exhausted, we hurried to the tornado shelter below the main passenger lounge and huddled there, together with the general and the commercial airline passengers. No one, including the airline pilots, could believe that we had just landed in such a storm.

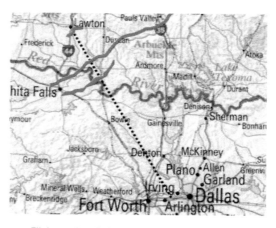

Flight track to Ft Sill and the thunderstorm lines

Our commander had given us up for dead but when he learned that we had survived, he assigned us to fly a Huey helicopter the next day supporting disaster recovery. The destruction was everywhere. Looking back, I consider it a wise decision to fly so soon after this experience because if I'd had time to think about it, I might never have flown again.

A week or so later, we retrieved 089 and flew it to the airplane bone yard at Davis–Monthan Air Force Base in Arizona. The aircraft had been damaged so bad that it was not economically feasible to repair and return to normal service.

Besides retiring the aircraft, there was also fallout of an official nature. The G-1 was quite upset at having come so close to death and he requested that the Pentagon Inspector General investigate the "incident". The board of investigators commended the pilots but a few months later the unit commander was quietly retired from active duty. The investigators held him responsible for sending out a plane into such a violent storm without having adequate or working radar equipment.

Radar data measured the storm that we flew into as reaching over 54,000 feet high. The resulting damage in Lawton and Wichita Falls, Texas was devastating. Twelve people were killed in Lawton; sixty-nine died in Wichita Falls. The Lawton airport remained closed for days because of the damage. One of the fatalities occurred when a car was tossed from a road. Called "Terrible Tuesday" by many meteorologists, the tornado that struck Lawton, destroyed over 116 structures and damaged over 330 others. Unanchored homes were completely swept from their foundations.

In all my flying career, either before or after, I had never been in an airplane so completely out of control, so certain that I would die, and so grateful to be wrong on all accounts. I flew through a CAT 5 thunderstorm and lived to fly another day.

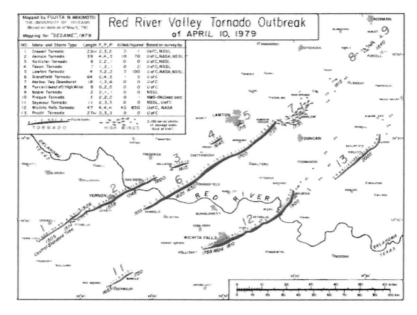

Tornado Line on April 10, 1979

REMEMBER WHEN: ... NOBODY BELIEVED WEATHER FORECASTS EXCEPT THE FORECASTERS...

"... WELL, TELL THAT ☼⚡☺☆≢△◖☆, WE'LL TAKE A SPECIAL VFR OUT OF HERE..."

" ...SOMETHING TELLS ME, WE SHOULD CANCEL THIS FLIGHT... "

ARMY 261

Army C-12, Tail number N22261

During the mid-1980s, American and French relations were strained, and military members assigned to Europe were required to obtain French visas as a form of diplomatic protest—pawns in a global game. When off duty military members wanted to tour Paris and see the sights, the length of time and attitude of French bureaucrats processing the visa requests led to a lot of frustration and last-minute changes in vacation plans. The French military, on the other hand, seemed generally cooperative and we routinely overflew France on our way to Beirut to supply the Marines deployed there. Overflight merely took a request coordinated in advance which was known as a diplomatic approval. Diplomatic approval was easy, but if you had to land in France, it was a different story.

Added to holding visas hostage, there were reports of French weapons being sold to Lebanese groups who were actively targeting the

Marines and other US interests in Beirut. The French government vigorously denied the reports of French weapons being sold, but the reporting continued and from what we were hearing it was hard to dismiss.

At the direction of decision makers well above my pay grade and with the information available to the Army, I was selected to fly a mission using my Army fixed wing detachment C-12 (Beechcraft B200) to transport a squad of Army Rangers to suspected weapons factory located on an airfield in France. I was asked to make it look like a normal training flight, land and once on the ground, park as close to the factory as possible. There would be no diplomatic approval, no flight plan and we would be carrying a heavily armed raiding party of six Special Operations, US Army Rangers. We were to sneak them into and out of France without alerting either French Air Traffic Control or the French military. We were quite literally invading France with an armed, American force.

To make this work, we prepared and filed a standard training flight plan to the Netherlands. And since it is used around the world as both a government and civilian business airplane, the C-12 was not likely to draw much attention with its standard white paint and lack of military markings.

We discretely loaded the "passengers" into the cabin and took off from our airport in West Germany. We climbed to an initial cruising altitude of 24,000 feet. Air traffic control in Germany was always excellent, and that day proved no exception. The flight was cleared without delay, and I flew a normal flight path while in German airspace towards the Netherlands. The mission had begun.

In the passenger seats sat a Special Forces Captain and his raiding party, all dressed in camouflage, combat gear, with weapons at the ready. They were silent and pensive. Some were carefully adjusting their weapons. Some were simply sitting still. One or two showed their apprehension by fidgeting with nervous energy.

Just prior to being transferred to Dutch ATC in Maastricht, we cancel our flight plan and ask the German controllers for permission to descend for some low-level training and flight using visual flight rules. ATC approved our request. We began descending at 1,500 feet per minute to just above tree top level. I intended to fly a nap-of-the-earth to avoid radar detection if possible. We pulled out our maps, turned off the transponder and navigation lights, and began one of the most challenging flights of my career. Our steep descent signalled the start of something irreversible, possibly dangerous, and as far as I was aware, completely without precedence. "La Fayette," I thought to myself, "the Americans are here."

We maintained strict radio silence but kept a listening watch on the international emergency VHF "Guard" frequency of 121.5. There was an air of anticipation in the plane as the raiding party conducted pre-combat checks of their equipment, reviewed diagrams of the facility and attempted to leave nothing to chance. While keenly aware that they were not flying into a hostile country or entering combat; they were, in fact, unannounced and uninvited in France to find evidence of illegal weapons sales.

As we flew at tree top level toward the French border as fast and as low as the plane could safely fly, I noted the time, 09:45. It would be another hour before we reached the target airport. We continued to streak below the trees and across the low-lying farmlands of the Champagne Region. Farmers looked up from their ploughs, women paused while hanging out their washing, and startled horses stampeded across open fields. The Guard frequency was quiet, we were still undetected.

We used an indirect route towards the airport so that if we were identified on radar our actual destination might not be evident. As we neared the airport, we monitored the control tower and climbed to traffic-pattern-altitude approximately 1500 feet above the ground. We slowed to normal traffic-pattern airspeed all the while feigning radio failure. No one seemed to take notice. The tower controllers asked in French what our intentions were, so we flashed the landing lights as the international signal of radio failure but did not respond. The tower cleared us to land by a half-hearted flashing of a green light signal: cleared to land. The ruse worked and we landed on a beautiful clear day without communication or incident.

Target Airport (2008)

The raiding party's target was a weapons factory with access to the airfield. After touchdown we taxied as rapidly as possible to a parking ramp close to the factory; ignoring the normal transient parking denoted by a large yellow 'C' sign. We shut the engines down, the crew chief opened the door, and the team began to move rapidly towards the factory. The men sprinted across the open ramp to the factory entrance with their weapons carried in a non-threatening but ready manner. The sound was impressive; six men running as one without a word, just the swish of clothing and clanking of equipment as they moved. The factory door was unlocked and the team entered without a confrontation.

The raiding party was in and out in a matter of minutes and without much notice. They came back with a sheaf of documents and three weapons boxes full of French L-59 machine guns. The documents indicated that the weapons were bound for Beirut. It was time to take off as quickly as possible.

My co-pilot started the number two engine while the team quickly loaded the weapons boxes. Without calling tower or permission, we began to taxi to the runway and took off. The cabin was heavy with the sound of relieved soldiers breathing normally again. Within minutes of take-off there were cheers, animated conversation and laughter, a symptom of relief from a very tense situation. We were happy in the cockpit too; and when one of the lads brought a machine gun up for a photo opportunity, we couldn't help but "ham" it up for the camera. The whole ground operation had taken only minutes to carry out.

Despite the relief of getting there and off the ground safely, we were far from home as we still had to contend with flying out of France. We took a different route out for our escape and kept watch for the French fighters which I was sure would appear. Would they find us, force us to land or just shoot us down? Amazingly, we heard nothing on the VHF emergency frequency radio. The minutes ticked by............

We flew low and fast towards Switzerland along the German-Swiss border staying below the trees and using valleys whenever possible, making our way back to the safety of German airspace. When we crossed the border into Germany, we were elated as we climbed to normal altitude. German ATC was more than happy to provide clearance back to our home airfield. We were surprised when they asked us if we'd had good hunting. Upon return to our airport, the Rangers thanked us and returned to their base. The weapons and documents were processed, and we were to keep our "training flight" quiet for years to come.

As suspected, there was no immediate French reaction to the raid. According to all reports, the French government was not even sure who had come in and taken the weapons, but the requirement for an American visa into France disappeared soon after our raid and relations between American and France thawed. Sometime after the raid an eight-foot-high chain link fence was quietly erected to protect the arms factory and separate the aircraft ramp and taxiway from further incursions.

CW2 Randall with one of the captured French L-59 Machine Guns

BOSS 88

I flew C-12s in Germany for five years at the height of the Cold War, during the Reagan era. Each day seem to bring a new adventure. I had the privilege of flying many high-ranking officers and dignitaries including many generals, a future Secretary of State, Colin Powell, and a future Supreme Allied Commander of Europe, General George Joulwan.

Personally autographed photo: "To Craig Randall – With deep appreciation and respect for his countless contributions to V Corps, SOUTHCOM, his country and to all. Best wishes to the best pilot in Army Aviation."
Signed: George A. Joulwan, GEN, USA, SACEUR

Left to Right: CW3 Craig Randall, Craig's Copilot, Hon Casper
Weinberger (Secretary of Defense), Craig's Crew Chief

I became a Berlin Corridor Instructor Pilot in the C-12 and U-21,
flying the same routes and procedures that had been established in
1948-49 to break the Soviet blockade and helped to save Berlin from
starvation. Until the reunification of Germany in 1989, those procedures and limited routes were the only way in and out of West Berlin
which was 119 miles inside East Germany by air and a Soviet controlled,
communist country—an enemy of the United States.

Occasionally, Soviet MiG fighters would intercept us during our
flights through the corridors, and it was pretty intense because we
didn't know whether or not a MiG pilot might decide to shoot us down.
While it hadn't happened since the 50's, the Russians had shot down at
least one airplane in the corridor, so the threat was real. Aircraft were
controlled by the Berlin Air Route Traffic Control Center (BARTCC)
and monitored by the Berlin Air Safety Center. Air traffic controllers
seemed to take great delight in telling American pilots the position of

the MiG's and how they were rolling in on them in an attack profile from far above and behind. I always hoped that the Russians were just practicing their intercept techniques. While they might be having fun, it scared the crap out of me each and every time it happened.

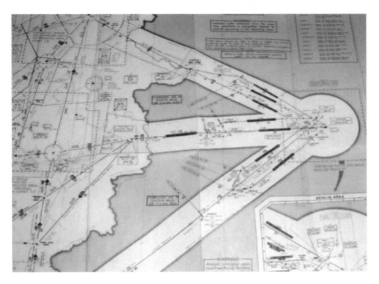

Berlin Corridor Instrument Flight Rules aeronautical chart, 1980s

Our normal destination in Berlin was Tempelhof Air Base. It was an incredible experience to see the massive aerodrome built just prior to World War II, by Albert Speer, Hitler's master architect.

Tempelhof Airbase, 1980s

Tempelhof was designed to showcase Nazi supremacy. As a child, I had watched movies of the big Douglas C-54 Skymasters, which my Uncle Byrle had flown, bringing in supplies to the cut-off city, drifting down between the apartment houses and landing safely over and over again.

It was in this environment that I was asked to fly a group of officers so they could see Mahlwinkle airfield, a Soviet airbase visible within the corridor track. These officers wanted to photograph and record any activity at the airbase. Why they wanted to do this was not explained and the less I knew, the better I felt. To get the picture meant flying to Berlin Tempelhof Airport using the center corridor. Flying the center corridor was a little unusual because Army airplanes normally flew the south corridor to Berlin and then departed Berlin towards Frankfurt using the central corridor. I was told that they needed to photograph the Russian airfield but wanted to use a recognizable VIP airplane so as not to raise suspicion. The mission was approved by the chain of command and I was to be the pilot in command to make it happen.

I had heard rumours of some C-12s with modifications to take pictures covertly, but our VIP planes did not. My challenge would be to fly the aircraft in such a manner as to allow photographic activity out of a passenger window flying a maneuver known as a slip, without raising Soviet suspicions. We couldn't change speed, heading, or altitude when we were over the airfield, because the Soviets had monitors in the allied air traffic facilities to keep track of all activity. But the monitors could only see our transponder and radar "blip," they couldn't see the actual angle of the airplane. Performing a slip is a maneuver every pilot is taught in initial training but is not common in a C-12. In a slip, the pilot uses an excessive amount of rudder to fly the airplane with one wing dipped at a steep angle while keeping the airplane on the

Example of flying in a side slip

heading, track and altitude. A slip is not an aerobatic maneuver, but it is a little uncomfortable for the passengers as you are flying the airplane well out of trim and definitely not straight and level. A slip would make sure that we would not be reported by the Soviets for unusual maneuvering over the base.

We would also fly slower than normal for the entire trip in the central corridor and all the minimum corridor altitudes so that when we were over the airbase, I could easily slip the airplane and give my

31

passengers the optimum vantage point of the target. Because we had two pilots flying, I even managed to take a few of my own "happy snaps".

Personal photos of Mahlwinkel Airbase pasted together to make a photographic mosaic

I was nervous doing this "spy work" for the first time, but we were successful. Not a peep out of the Russian observers in the ATC facility. And, our passengers were so happy with how easy it was, we repeated it many times; always in the guise of flying VIPs into Berlin so as not to rouse the Soviet air traffic monitors.

Because of these flights, I was asked to do something a little more "adventurous" by the same organization some time later in my tour. I was asked to fly a similar photo-reconnaissance mission using our VIP C-12. This time, the target was a new Soviet anti-aircraft missile battery near Belgrade, Yugoslavia. We were well beyond a typical Berlin Corridor mission.

Operating as 'Boss 88' with the Detachment Commander as my co-pilot, we would fly deep into the 'Iron Curtain' — well over 400 nautical miles — into Soviet controlled airspace, to the Communist controlled country of Yugoslavia. This time, we were going to operate as an American government delegation working to re-establish ties with Yugoslavia.

The "delegation" we were flying were dressed in stripped down military uniforms with only rank and collared shirt with ties—no nametags, awards or decorations. The delegation had meetings set up in Belgrade, but the only goal was to photograph the missile launching sites.

It would be a challenge to achieve the success on this mission as we had so easily done along the Berlin corridor because of the distance, hostile ATC, general suspicions between East and West as well as the actual location of the target well off of any route to and from Belgrade. The site was located northeast of our planned return flight, which the Soviets had to approve in advance of our actual flight. It was going to be hard to conceal our intentions once we started to deviate and any other activity was simply a ruse to conceal the purpose of our mission. At all cost we diverted attention away from the aircraft to make it appear that we were indeed in Yugoslavia for negotiations between our two countries.

The flight to Belgrade was uneventful and we stayed at the Soviet owned and run 'Mokba Hotel' in downtown Belgrade. I was later informed that the Soviets always had a 'Mokba Hotel' and restaurant in all their satellite countries and that we should expect that our rooms had listening devices, that we could be followed and were most certainly under some form of surveillance.

When we arrived, we actually had a good time as there was a well-stocked bar to frequent, a casino to gamble in and beautiful and historic sites within Belgrade to tour. But, from the outside, what was considered to be the leading hotel in Belgrade, the Mokba was an uninspired, grey, drab, dull Communist structure with overbearing staff and nosy people everywhere.

While waiting for the "negotiations" to conclude, we made it a game to try and pick out our surveillance and it wasn't really that hard. The Soviet spies were easy to pick out as they dressed in ill-fitting gray suits and wore trilby hats just like the spies in bad B grade movies. Locals didn't use the hotel casino either, so it appeared to be reserved just for foreign male guests. I say male guest because the place was full of willing female companions, who were distinguishable by their red dresses, bored expressions, and hefty thighs. They also came and went to various rooms on a revolving basis.

After several days of "negotiations," we made our preparations to fly back to Germany, during which time the passengers in back would accomplish their real task; the photographing of anti-aircraft missile sites northeast of Belgrade.

Our plan was actually quite simple; we would fake both communications and navigation equipment problems. The hope was that we would be perceived as having real problems until we accomplished our true mission.

As we took off, we flew a normal flight path until we came near our target area where I began to 'drift' off-course to bring the cameras within a better range of the missile batteries. The "diplomats" prepared their photographic equipment by taking it out of a panel in the baggage compartment that had been installed just for this mission. While I slowly drifted off-course nearer to the target area, it occurred to me that one of their pictures could include an enemy missile fired at us, but I didn't dwell on it as we did not have any defensive equipment nor could our aircraft out maneuver a missile. As I pushed those thoughts away, my heartbeat increased and my copilot and I became very quiet. We knew that this mission had some risks and we expected to take a few chances to get the photographs.

Belgrade Approach Control began calling us almost immediately as they recognized our plane drifting off-course.

'Boss 88, you are off-course, turn left twenty degrees.'

'Belgrade, this is Boss 88, say again, we are having radio difficulty, say again please.'

'Boss 88, turn left now, you are off-course. Turn left ninety degrees.'

At the same time as this dialogue was taking place with Belgrade Approach, the "diplomats" were shouting at me from the back of the plane.

'We can see it! We can see it! Keep the right wing down we're getting great shots!'

Meanwhile, the Russian controllers were going berserk, demanding that we contact Zagreb approach immediately for better radio contact. By then, we were more than fifteen miles east of track, way off course. We took our time contacting the Zagreb controllers and when we did, they told us in very firm terms to turn left 90 degrees and proceed direct to Zagreb for an immediate landing. We were also warned that Zagreb had launched fighters to intercept us and escort our plane for "landing and inspection."

When the MiG 21 sidled up alongside our C-12, I had no choice but to comply with the controllers or risk being shot down. The Soviets were serious about the intercept. I shouted to our enthusiastic photographers that we were being forced to land at Zagreb and that they should get ready for a really thorough inspection. They calmly began hiding their equipment. The MiG escorted us right to the runway end as we landed, then circled and came in to land after we did. We were met by military vehicles on the ground and during our taxi, we were "escorted" to a deserted corner of the main parking area at the nearly empty Zagreb airport. As we shut down the engines we were met by a small and hostile reception party waiting under the shade of some trees.

Example of intercepting MiG 21

I hoped that my fear was not showing but I was really worried now. We kept up the pretence of being an American delegation and even managed to show outrage that our VIP passengers were being inconvenienced, lest they all might be locked up and the proverbial key thrown away.

An armed boarding party was waiting to search the aircraft. The delegation took their time getting off the plane and complained all the while about what a travesty the situation was and threatening loudly that the incident would have serious diplomatic repercussions. The "diplomats" were slowly escorted over to the edge of the ramp and stood in the shade of one of the trees previously used by the armed boarding party. Surprisingly, no one bothered to guard I or my copilot. They were only interested in the aircraft and were searching it enthusiastically.

With my copilot staying with the airplane, I was escorted over to the airport command center by an armed guard. I was questioned for about an hour as to why I'd been off course. I stuck to the story that our equipment had shown we were on course, and I couldn't explain why we were off-course. I told them maybe it was a failure in their equipment. I was trying to play it cool, but I wasn't too sure how I was doing. But I stuck to the story regardless of how many different ways they asked me the same questions.

I had to admit that the show of weapons and the aggressiveness of the aircraft search and questioning, not to mention the MiG intercept of a diplomatic aircraft, had my mind racing with all sorts of unpleasant possibilities. I hoped like hell that we would pull the ruse off because I really wanted to see my family again. Meanwhile, as they were questioning me, back at the plane our 'hosts' searched each piece of baggage, every inch of the airplane, and found absolutely nothing. Because this was a diplomatic mission, they could not do a strip search of everyone on board without any evidence of violating international diplomatic rules. Thankfully or luckily, we did not give them a justification to hold us or demand a strip search, so after several hours, we were released and allowed to depart. In very clear and uncertain terms we were told to leave the country and not have any other navigation or communication problems on the way out. We took off as fast as we could and headed back to the West.

Personal Pilot Logbook entry of Imagery Reconnaissance and
MIG 21 intercept in Yugoslavia

Landing back at our airport later that night, we bid the "diplomats" a final goodbye, finished our duties and went home. I never heard anything about the photos they took or whether the payoff was worth the risk. What I do know is that I was happy being back in a free country and never wanted to be intercepted by a hostile aircraft again.

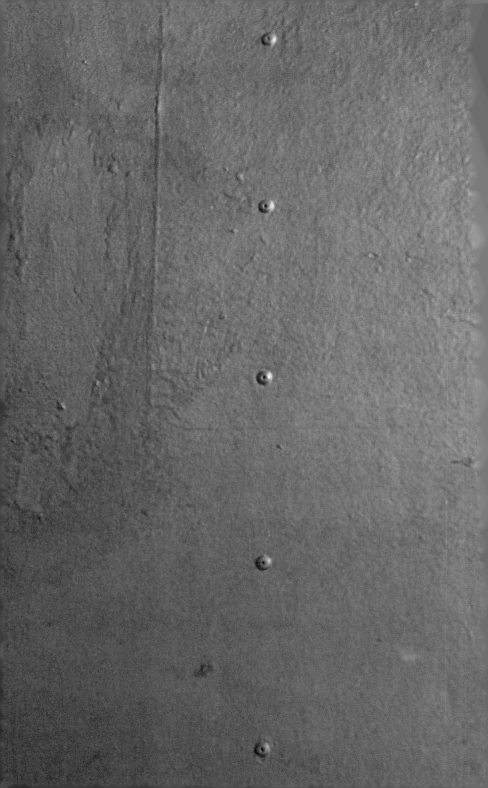

BLACK 5

When President Ronald Reagan launched the "War on Drugs" and declared illicit drugs to be a threat to our national security, the US Army South (USARSO) operating in Central and South America added drug interdiction as a new task to its list of responsibilities. By the time I was assigned to Bravo Company, 1st Battalion of the 228th Aviation Regiment at Howard Air Force Base, Panama in 1991, our little fleet of C-12s were involved in that war in ways I never imagined.

Shortly after my arrival, I was given an Alert Order as the pilot in command of a C-12 mission to support Operation "Promote Liberty." Operation Promote Liberty was the name given to all post Operation Just Cause civil-military missions. "Promote Liberty" was supposed to help stabilize the region after Panamanian Leader General Manual Noriega's capture. "Promote Liberty" was designed to support the president's drug interdiction mandate in Central and South America, support the new Panamanian government and restore basic services in Panama.

My co-pilot for this flight would be the USARSO Chief of Staff, a staff officer and a Lieutenant Colonel. Our flight was going to support the drug interdiction part of the mission. The mission would be to pick up a Special Operations Forces (SOF) team, which was already in the area.

I walked into my commander's office to get the details of the mission. The B Company Commander explained that there was a new runway in the Amazon jungle with a DC-3 sitting next to what appeared to be a cocaine production facility along the Amazon basin in Colombia. The commander's guidance for the flight was to assist the SOF Team. We would allow the team to conduct a visual reconnaissance from our C-12, and; if the plane and drugs were at the site, drop the team off back at an airport close by and wait for them. The SOF team would hike through the jungle to the suspect site, destroy everything they found and defend themselves against any resistance they encountered. Once the mission was complete, the team would hike back to the airport where we would be waiting to pick them up. We would then fly ourselves and the team back to Howard AFB in Panama. Our call sign would be Black 5.

DC-3 at an undisclosed jungle airstrip in Colombia

Although it sounded straight forward, due to the distance, mission length and austere facilities, refueling would be required at Bogota on the way down to the Amazon region and again on the way back to Howard AFB. Someone else had coordinated all the diplomatic clearances to fly to Colombia, so I spent the rest of the day planning the mission, fuel, weight and balance and other details necessary for success. Satisfied with my planning, I went to bed dreaming of everything that could go wrong on this mission.

The day started with a 5am wake up, breakfast and weather briefing. I went to our hangar to link up with my copilot. My copilot was trying to get his monthly flying hours in and I wasn't sure if he was aware of what we would be doing. I thought that it would be an exciting day for him as staff guys never got to do the long, harder missions. Since I was the Check Airman (Standardization Instructor Pilot in Army lingo) and Pilot in Command, I told my copilot that he would fly to Bogota and then to the Amazon basin. I would fly the reconnaissance mission and the remaining legs to Panama later that night. The plan was to depart Howard at 7am and fly to Bogota, Colombia to refuel. Then, fly further south to the Amazon basin as close as we could get to the target in Colombia on the border with Ecuador. Since it was 'wet season'

General route of flight from Panama to Colombia and back

in Panama, we discussed our options if we needed to deviate around any storms. I, my copilot and the enlisted crew chief departed on time and flew without incident to Bogota, where we refueled and then continued the flight to the Amazon basin.

We landed at the airport nearest the target and taxied over to a dilapidated tin hut and shut down. Six SOF team members emerged from the jungle, fully armed. I met the Detachment Commander (Det CO), a young, sharp junior officer. We shook hands and he got his map out to discuss the reconnaissance. We would take off and fly west low level down the Amazon River without a flight plan, in visual conditions. All six team members would ride along to get an image of their target so the team could more accurately plan their ingress, egress and attack assuming the plane and drugs were there.

Amazon basin near the target (2006 picture)

We loaded up the aircraft, and everyone strapped in except the Det CO, who calmly stood between the two pilot seats and said he was ready. I asked him to sit down and he said no. I added power and we took off down the remote strip.

Almost up to the turn of the century, the Amazon basin was a real wild West. It was part of many countries who shared the border, but for the most part it was only governed by various "outlaw" groups fighting the governments and each other for control of the coca crop and distribution. The rules there were different and there were plenty of locals watching for both the good guys and the bad guys.

To keep our true intentions secret and not alert the bad guys, we flew at about three hundred feet above the ground following the river for about fifty miles. Once we felt certain that our true destination was still a secret, we made our way surreptitiously towards the target area. As we rounded a wide corner in the river headed towards the target area, a shout came from one of the SOF guys in the back that he saw the target at our two o'clock on the right hand side. I rolled into a right bank to give them all a better look, and as I did, tracer rounds began coming up from the jungle towards the aircraft. Team members called out the incoming small arms fire, and I pulled up into a low cloud base at about fifteen hundred feet. Adrenaline pumping, I was surprised at how rapid and intense the ground fire had been. I was thankful it wasn't very accurate.

The senior Noncommissioned Officer came up to stand next to the Det CO. He asked me if his team could shoot through the small side passenger windows located on both sides of the cabin. I told him no because there would be too much chance of hitting a propeller if firing forward, or an engine or the wing if they became too focused on the target to say nothing of the brass ricocheting around the cockpit.

I was now circling at about sixteen hundred feet using the clouds to camouflage our flight path. Even as the clouds were protecting us, they were also hiding all the ground details, so I started a descent back out of the clouds. They were thin enough that at about five hundred feet above the ground, I started another run towards the target airstrip.

Once again, we started taking ground fire from the jungle, but I placed my faith in the assumption "Big sky, little bullet" and prayed we would not be shot down. The team members began shouting details that would help them with their raid:

"DC-3 on the far end of the dirt strip, being loaded!"

"Cocaine facility!"

"Good beach to land on South of the runway!"

"Ten guns firing at us!"

After several anxious minutes, they started saying "Got it!" "Got it!" At that point, the Det CO calmly asked me to return us to local airport. We made another circuitous route towards the airport flying no higher than three hundred feet. Once it was in sight, we landed and taxied back to the tin hut that served as the FBO where there was a section of Colombian soldiers loitering. The team deplaned without a word and disappeared into the jungle. The Det CO said they would be back in about three hours and that we should be ready to go in a hurry.

I and my copilot waited in the sweltering heat. I had a nine-millimeter Beretta and a 22-caliber pistol, my copilot had his Beretta as well and our crew chief had an M-16. Not really enough fire power compared to what we had just flown through and we had little confidence that the Colombians would be of any help either. If some narcos decided to engage us, it would have been a very short firefight and we would have been on the losing end. We put those thoughts aside and wandered over to the shack where a lady was cooking for the soldiers and the locals. We bought some cold sodas to help us calm down and wait on the team.

Black 5 at airport near the tin shack: Army 85-51269
(Later crashed in the Brazilian jungle)

Almost to the minute, three hours after they disappeared, the SOF team emerged from the jungle. They were quiet, pensive, and far dirtier than when they had left. Little was said as we climbed aboard the aircraft and departed. They were all back safely.

Flying back to Bogota to refuel, the Det CO gave me a rundown on the assault. The DC-3 was destroyed and burning on the runway. The entire coca production facility was destroyed and burning. No team members were wounded or injured. The only thing he mentioned about the narcos is that they tried to prevent the assault and that they were poorly trained and disciplined. I never asked if they had to kill anyone and he didn't volunteer. Probably better not to know that detail. All and all, mission accomplished. With his job done, the Det CO finally went to the cabin and sat down, he could relax.

As we climbed up and out of the airport, weather had cleared up so that when we overflew the attack site at a safe altitude, I could easily see the smoke from two distinct fires rising from the jungle. The men in back quietly looked out the windows at their work. It had been a long and dangerous day.

While we refueled in Bogota, the team found a small office and restroom to clean up. With full tanks and a refreshed team, we flew in the dark of night dodging the ever present thunderstorms while everyone quietly mulled over what they had just gone through. We landed at 10pm local time back in Panama. The team went their way and we went to our quarters.

Black 5 had quite a day. We flew 7.7 flight hours of which almost two hours were in the clouds. We made 5 landings, two of which were instrument landings at El Dorado International Airport in Bogota and had an 18 hour duty day. We had flown tactically, been shot at and put ourselves in harm's way to give the SOF team the info it needed to conduct a successful raid. If it had been a declared war, we could have been awarded Air Medals and other valor decorations. But the War on Drugs was not something that made for heroes and glory. Our only reward was to land safely and be excused from duty the following day.

As fixed wing aviators, we had it pretty easy compared to our SOF team counterparts. But for both pilots and SOF, that day was about duty and professionalism. There would be no newspaper headlines and no one asking what we were doing blowing up airplanes and buildings in the jungles of South America. Just doing the job asked of us. An intense and dangerous, but very interesting job.

CYCLOPS 41

When most people think of Operation Desert Shield / Desert Storm, they remember the images on CNN: Huge explosions in Bagdad, M1 tanks advancing through the desert and multiple rocket launchers shooting missiles trailing plumes of arching smoke. Few, if any remember or know of the participation of a Vietnam legend, the Grumman OV-1 Mohawk.

The OV-1 entered production in October 1959 and was fielded to US Army airplane units starting in 1961. The single pilot aircraft had multiple mission configurations. It was equipped with ejection seats for the pilot and intelligence equipment operator called a Technical Observer or "T.O." for short. It was fully aerobatic and built like a tank. Roughly 380 were built and the OV-1 saw combat in the Vietnam War while assigned to five surveillance companies. These units lost 65 Mohawks to accidents, antiaircraft fire, ground fire and one shot down by a North Vietnamese fighter. The aircraft also saw many victories supporting ground operations as well as one confirmed shoot down of a North Vietnamese fighter. After Vietnam, the Mohawks were assigned duty around the world with units in Korea, Germany, and the USA. They saw cold war service along the intra-borders of East and West Germany and North and South Korea. Until the arrival of the Air Force JSTARS, the OV-1 was the only airborne moving target indicator surveillance technology with a proven battlefield record. When planning the ground assault in what would be known as Desert Storm, the Army wanted its capabilities for operations against Iraq. With the fall of the wall and end of the Soviet Union and reunification of East and West Germany in 1989, The Army ordered the 2nd Military Intelligence Battalion, out of Stuttgart, Germany to deploy to an airbase in Saudi Arabia. The unit started flying day and night to develop the Iraqi order of battle.

Life was fairly safe as we flew in Saudi airspace prior to the war and then over Iraq when the Iraqi Air Force had been destroyed.

The most excitement we had was the Scud missile alerts and attacks which happened more often that anyone wished.

CPT AB flying the OV-1 Mohawk

Once the Operation Desert Storm attack started, we pushed even harder to support the ground forces. Burning oil clouds caused problems with visibility and we also learned to deal with the sandstorms. It was a harsh flying environment, but we were in combat and would not let anyone down. With the battle going our way and the Iraqis falling back so rapidly, we knew that we were stretching our capabilities in distances flown and time on station to keep pace.

My mission on February 28th, 1991 started normally. A two-ship late-night surveillance mission inside Iraq to update our intelligence picture on the status the Iraqi forces. The distance and length of the mission increased the risk and both weather and fuel would be something to watch as the mission unfolded. The first aircraft took off before us and would therefore return first. With all the activity on the ground, I expected it would be a busy night.

Even prior to take-off, the weather at the airbase was becoming a bit hazy which was a big change from the crystal-clear nights we had become accustom. More disconcerting was the fact that we had no weather forecasters assigned to the airbase. Our weather briefings were done over the phone with weather forecasters based at King Khalid Air Base (KKAB) some fifty miles away and might as well have been on another planet.

We were given the call sign Cyclops 41. With all the prefight paperwork complete, and a valid weather forecast, we launched for another long combat sortie.

The mission that night was mostly routine, but the haze at the airfield kept gnawing at me, so as was our in-house procedure, I called back to the airport and talked with the Ground Control Approach (GCA) team that provided us with our instrument approach capability. The GCA controller told me that the weather was "OK" when I called to check. The mission was going well, and I would continue to call GCA about every 30 minutes or so just to stay on the safe side.

We conducted a relief on station with another aircraft and departed Iraq. Clearing the combat zone and switching from our AWACS battlefield controllers to the airfield GCA controllers I was shocked to hear the first Mohawk still in the air being vectored for what I thought was just a practice approach. It was not. I checked in with the controller and asked again about the weather. I received the same "It's OK" replay that I had been hearing all night. With the first Mohawk still trying to land, I knew differently.

I was approaching the city and should have been able to see plenty of lights, tonight there was nothing but darkness. I challenged the control about the OK weather report and asked him if he had really gone outside the building and looked at the weather. After a quick "standby," I got the response, "We didn't know it was this bad." On the GCA frequency, I had been monitoring the first Mohawk's approach and heard the pilot announce "missed approach." He was going around to try again. Definitely not the weather we had been promised.

What I didn't know was the other OV-1 crew was vectored by the GCA controller into a windsock which they hit with one of the wings while doing their approach. So, they were having controllability issues which I also was not aware of. As they vectored the first Mohawk around, it was now my turn to try and land. On my first approach I was taken all the way to decision height at which time I broke out of the clouds but was not anywhere near the airfield. At 200 feet above the ground, I could vaguely make out runway lights about a quarter mile or so off to my left. It was unsafe to try and make the runway from what the GCA controller had vectored, so I had to also call missed approach and executed a go round.

Being a quarter mile from the centerline of the runway, I was never on course like GCA claimed. Same was true for the first Mohawk which was why he hit the windsock. During my vectors for approach number two, I took a moment to radio King Khalid to ask what their weather conditions were like. The U.S. military controllers responded by saying it was "0-0." King Khalid had weather all the way down to the ground and no visibility to see your hand in front of your face, a real pea soup. King Khalid also indicated they had aircraft on the runway that were being towed into parking spots because they didn't have the visibility to taxi safely. The last thing they said was: "Don't come here."

With nowhere else to go, I figured since I did break out on my first approach, just not on course, that I would be able to make it on the second attempt. The initial GCA controller had been replaced by a more experienced controller so I was trying to be positive that I'd be on the ground on this approach. Unfortunately, my positive outlook was not rewarded. The first Mohawk, due to his controllability problems from hitting the windsock, crashed on the runway. Even though he had messed up his landing gear, had flat tires and bent props from the impact, he was still able to apply full-power to the engines and motor the damaged aircraft off the runway so that I could land. Besides all the physical damage the airplane sustained, his radios were also damaged in the crash. He could not tell tower or I that he had cleared the runway. With visibility so bad and no communication from the crashed airplane, the tower could not see him. I was told the runway was closed until they could figure out what was going on and I was denied permission to land.

After two missed approaches and all the vectoring, I knew that we were out of fuel: A real emergency on my hands. The crash shut down the only runway that I had any fuel or chance of landing on. While I was thankful the crew was okay, the runway had fire and rescue equipment on it cleaning up the wreckage and the controllers could not give me an estimate for when the runway would reopen. All they would say was: "Standby."

I knew that we didn't have much fuel and that within minutes, we could actually lose one or both engines due to fuel starvation. Thankfully, even though I was out fuel, I wasn't out of options. I estimated that I had as little as five minutes of fuel, so I told the T.O. that we would have to eject.

As calmly as I could, I informed ATC of my fuel status and requested vectors away from the airfield, over open desert, and away from friendly troops. I did not want to compound the emergency situation by having an airplane crash on top of somebody. While ATC worked on finding me a place to eject, I told the T.O. to jettison the Plexiglas over-head canopy (the top of the cockpit) so that we could eject without hitting anything on the way out. The TO replied that the canopy wouldn't come off. After several attempts to get the canopy to release using the canopy jettison handle, we tried to punch it loose with our fists, but it wouldn't budge. Fortunately, Grumman selected a Martin-Baker ejection seat and it was designed so that you could eject through the canopy. The ejection seat design and our flight helmets combined with the force of the ejection would break the canopy. The ejection seat had an upper and lower ejection handle. If you used the upper handle, a special face cover on the ejection handle would provide additional protection for our faces as we rocketed through the canopy.

The T.O., being about 19 years old or so, did not displaying any signs of nervousness. That young man had nerves of steel. I couldn't have had a more able man along with me that night to help prepare us and the aircraft for ejection. The moment after I gave him the command to eject, I saw a huge fireball leave the aircraft. He was out of the aircraft and gone. I had no contact with him after he ejected so I had no idea if he made it out alive or not. I remember thinking, "I hope I was not somehow the instrument of his death."

As the engines began to flame out, it was my turn. I told ATC I was ejecting and remember thinking: "If this ejection seat doesn't work, this could be the last few seconds of my life." I pulled the handle on the Martin-Baker ejection seat and blacked out from the G-forces.

My first conscience recollection was a great tug on my body as my parachute opened. It was so dark I could not see the ground. It seemed like I was floating downwards for a very long time when, suddenly, I hit the ground and was drug on my back until the parachute collapsed. It was so dark I could not see my hand in front of my face. I remember fumbling around my vest looking for my survival radio. I was able to contact a couple of Air Force A-10s that were already searching for the T.O. and I. The A-10s fixed our position and relayed to AWACS who relayed our position and status to our unit. Everyone was relieved to hear my voice. They told me that the T.O. had already checked in. He was alive. We were both on the ground, safe in Saudi Arabia.

Cyclops 41 the morning after ejecting

I had pain in my back and stomach, so I tried to just lay there in the blackness awaiting my rescuers. Around 3am, I started to see lights on the horizon. My rescuers and salvation were headed my way. Ground vehicles from my unit were arriving at my location. My rescuers were faces that I knew! I saw them jump off the vehicles and run towards me with looks of fear as they were thinking the worst. The looks turned to tears of joy when they saw I was alive. Our ordeal was over. We were rescued. The T.O. received minor facial injuries upon landing and was playing volleyball the next day. I received a spinal injury and was hospitalized at the 12th Army Evacuation Hospital. I eventually returned to flying after about a month.

Cyclops 41 the morning after ejecting

With the war successfully concluded, we redeployed back to our home base in Stuttgart, Germany. We came home to cheers and tears, family and unit celebrations and of course award ceremonies. Besides all the homecoming ceremonies, I was invited to one of the most unique award ceremonies in the world, the Martin Baker Ejection Seat Club.

The Ejection Tie Club was founded by Sir James Martin sometime after the ejection seat was created. The first pilot to be accepted into the Club was in January 1957.

Both I and my T.O. were treated to a visit to the Martin Baker headquarters in London, England to be inducted with the other pilots of the war who had successfully used their seats. It was a dress Blue event and to our surprise, Princess Diana was the guest of honor. She greeted each of us as we were presented our ejection seat tie, tie clip and certificate. Even though the exclusive club has over 6,000 registered members, I was the 4424th to safely eject. I am honored to be alive and a member of the club.

CPT AB meeting Princess Diana

While I have many memories of the war, the ejection and the homecoming, meeting the "fairy tale" Princess of England is definitely one of the highlights of my career and life.

"... GET YOUR LIE READY MIKE, HERE COMES TH' C.O., TH' X.O. AND THREE GERMAN FARMERS..."

NAIL 18

"**S**arge, tighten up your harness. I think it's going to get a little uncomfortable"....... And then the cockpit went dark, the windows froze over and the adventure began.

Looking back at what brought both of us to the eternity of the next five minutes of terror we were about to experience was nothing more than decisions made in youth, over confidence, and an ejection seat as an insurance policy. Because when you flew the Grumman OV-1D Mohawk in the 1990s, you were flying a war bird built by the company known as "The Iron Works." The Mohawk was a plane built to take a beating in combat and bring the single pilot and enlisted technical observer (the T.O.) back safely regardless of the situation or to eject using the insurance policy.

Nail 18 preparing for Indications and Warning Mission

I had been a rated fixed wing pilot for almost three years but only recently gotten back into the Mohawk. Even though I had over 1000 total flight hours, I had less than 300 hours flying airplanes when I took off that day. Korea was my first big Mohawk assignment, my first tour on the peninsula, and my first time flying a real world, critical mission known as Indications and Warnings: keeping an eye on North Korean ground activities so that there would not be any surprise attacks on South Korea. Our unit took the threat of a surprise attack seriously.

The cold war on the peninsula was in high gear, Kim Il-sung, the founding dictator of North Korea had recently died and his son and successor as leader, the late Kim Jong-il had publicly broadcast that he would bury his father in the capital of South Korea, Seoul. The Army had just upgraded its weapons as well by deploying multiple launch rocket system (MLRS) artillery units and the Patriot long-range, all-altitude, all-weather air defense system.

As the sabres rattled on both sides, we were tasked to fly much more than our normal number of missions. It wasn't too much of a hardship as most of the pilots and T.O.s were on one year "short tours" without families to see at the end of the day. Flying made the tour pass a little quicker and I was doing something I loved. So as I walked into operations to review the mission, update weather and complete the paperwork, it was just another hot, humid summer day on the ROK (Republic of Korea).

Our weather forecast was for hot, humid and windy weather with widespread thunderstorms developing up north, moving southeast along the peninsula. No big deal, nothing out of the ordinary and besides, we had a WX1000 Stormscope on board to detect lightning! We were briefed and authorized to fly the mission under instrument conditions, but it was mostly a visual flight conditions day. If worse came to worse, we could always deviate around the thunder-bumpers. Time to go earn a paycheck for God and country.

With the prefight complete, a quick run-up, taxi and number one for departure, we were off the ground on time and headed to what we commonly called "track." Track was merely the assigned route and altitude we would fly along the southern side of the Demilitarized Zone (DMZ). The majority of the track we would fly was inside a tactical airspace buffer zone (Tac Zone) that only military flights were authorized, and the airspace was controlled by military air traffic controllers. Track generally ran from the West coast to the East coast of the peninsula and paralleled the DMZ. After flying it back and forth until it was time to fly back to our airport both day and night, complacency could easily creep into any mission.

Somewhere along track, 1994

Track also had a singularly unique feature that limited both deviations and maneuvering, nicked named the "Key Hole" for its shape. The Keyhole was bounded by the DMZ which took an almost 180 degree turn near Seoul. To the South, Protected Airspace 73 (or Papa 73 in pilot speak) around the South Korean President's home (the "Blue House"). Papa 73 was protected by South Korean military that would happily shoot first and ask questions later if you inadvertently or deliberately wandered into their airspace. And, if that wasn't bad enough, the area was near and around the densely populated capital of Seoul. Trying to turn around in the narrowest part of the Keyhole left you playing Russian roulette with either the North Korean or South Korean military.

My mission started off routinely enough with a quick check-in with Seoul Approach for clearance to fly to the start point of the track. Flying out to the start point west of Seoul, the Yellow Sea was in view with the city of Incheon passing below us. You could see clouds building far north of our flight path, but nothing that was of any concern. We said goodbye to Seoul Approach and contacted the military controllers for approval to enter the Tac Zone and start our track. We were promptly cleared in and informed that there were a couple other aircraft in the Tac Zone at different altitudes and locations in relation to our track. Again, nothing unusual about that either. We entered the Tac Zone over the Yellow Sea and flew East. We would not reverse course to the West until over the Sea of Japan. Back and forth we would go until our fuel reached the Return To Base (RTB) point.

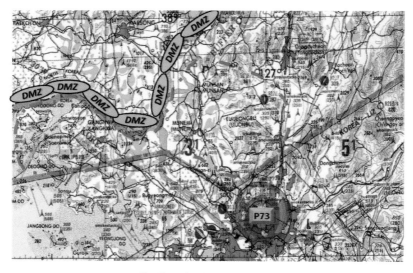

The Keyhole (Outlined in Red)

Once over the Sea of Japan, we made a southerly 180 degree turn to head back West. Much to our surprise, the clouds we had seen at the start of our track had now grown much larger and much more ominous than either of us expected. The T.O. and I discussed the weather for a while, but as the Stormscope was not picking up any activity to indicate lightning, onward we flew to continue our mission. We had time to reconsider and besides, we were in a Mohawk!

As Uijeongbu passed below us, it was clear that the building clouds were starting to develop into thunderstorms, but as the Stormscope was still quiet, I assumed it would be some heavy rain and some turbulence, nothing too terrible or serious to worry about. But the clouds now had my attention and I started asking Seoul Approach if they had any indications of thunderstorm activity. I received a very curt "negative" in English and nothing further. I called back to the military controllers for an update on weather around Seoul and they also said that while weather activity was building, they had no other information of things getting worse, so we stayed on track and started towards the Keyhole.

Committing to enter the Keyhole still gave us time to turn around if needed but as the Blue House and Papa 73 passed to the south of us and the DMZ got closer to us on the north side of the track, we were firmly committed to continue on track towards the start point over the Yellow Sea. As I looked up at the tops of the system, they were growing rapidly, exceeding 25,000 feet. So, it was going to be a little worse than I thought but shouldn't be too bad; I kept reassuring myself.

We went in and out of the first build up. It was bumpy. Raining inside the clouds. But, not too bad. We came out on the other side a minute or so later only to be staring at a fully developed Cumulonimbus towering above 30,000 feet with a well-developed anvil. The whole thing was directly over the narrowest part of the Keyhole and it appeared to cover the entire track north to south.

With your helmet on, visor down and oxygen mask on, you really can't read another's face, but we both looked at each other with a knowing "oh shit" look. So here we were. No way to reverse course, no idea what was lurking inside this monster and no indications on the Stormscope that there was any lightning activity to worry about. My inner voice had switched to overdrive and as we flew under the anvil, I saw the virga coming out of it. I said the only thing I could think of: "Sarge, tighten up your harness. I think it's going to get a little uncomfortable."

A towering Cumulonimbus similar to what we were looking at in the Keyhole

In more of a reaction than thought, I tightened up my own harness, turned all the lights in the cockpit to bright and said a quick prayer of desperation. In the time it took to do that, the outside world got very dark and even though it was July on the ground, it was cold enough at our altitude that as soon as we entered the cloud, the cockpit completely iced over. And if that wasn't bad enough, we hit the first bit of turbulence and it kicked off the autopilot. I was now flying what's known as basic instrument skills: heading, altitude and airspeed. For the first time in my flying career, I felt that I was in over my head and that there was a real danger that this storm could hurt us.

As I tried to concentrate on keeping the aircraft going in the right direction, at the right altitude and at the right airspeed, I felt it was a losing battle. As I worked the controls, one second, we were heading due north (a very bad thing) and climbing at 4000-5000 feet per minute. *"Pull the power back. Correct the heading to west,"* I told myself. The next second the turbulence pushed us back down at the same rate and we're heading almost due south (another bad thing). *"Push the power forward. Correct the heading back to west,"* I told myself. Over and over this scenario repeated itself. It seemed like we were on a runaway elevator with no way out. The voice in my head continued to repeat the mantra from flight school:

"Heading, altitude, airspeed."
Heading, altitude, airspeed."
Heading, altitude, airspeed."

As we were being bounced around by the storm, I could also hear the rain and the wind and the sheer energy of the storm.

"Heading, altitude, airspeed."
Heading, altitude, airspeed."
Heading, altitude, airspeed."

I chanted all the louder with my inner voice. And it if I didn't have enough excitement in my day, the thunder and lightning made it even more terrifying; thanks for the warning Mr. Stormscope!

The voice in my head was now telling me something panicky and the mantra had ceased.

"You're losing the airplane, it's time to eject!"

As I struggled to keep the airplane going where it was supposed to, I was now arguing with my inner voice:

"You want to eject in a thunderstorm? If the plane can't handle it, how well do you think a silk parachute will handle it?"

The voice suddenly quieted but I kept with my training.

"Heading, altitude, airspeed."
Heading, altitude, airspeed."
Heading, altitude, airspeed."

It seemed like the storm was never going to end, but as suddenly as it started, it stopped. We were still covered with ice as the window defroster tried in vain to melt it away. But it was calm. We were about 600 feet higher than our assigned altitude and heading slightly south of our intended track. I corrected both the heading and the altitude, put the autopilot back on and sat there trying to calm myself down so that I could talk to the T.O. We were both silent as we flew back towards our start point. We were supposed to turn around at the start point and make another trip down the track; not a pleasant thought at all.

As we approached the start point, I could finally see a little out of the cockpit. Weather up north was going to throw some more storms at us. I did not feel invincible anymore and the ejection seat would not be any help in the violence of a thunderstorm. I had clearly been humbled. I looked at the T.O. and told him we were done, time to go home, I won't temp fate twice. I could see the tension fade from his body and he simply said, "Oh, thank God."

The flight home took about twenty minutes and as the ice shed from the plane, I was wondering what the other pilots would think of me for returning early from the mission. In the macho world of the Mohawk pilot, would I be looked at as a less than professional pilot? But as we landed and parked, I realized that none of that really mattered because experience had blessed me, and I would never put myself in a predicament like that again.

My thoughts were still reviewing my actions when I was interrupted by the ground crew pointing at the leading edge ice that was still melting off the airplane. I completed my walk around and recorded that the number three accelerometer had been activated three times. While I'm not a maintenance guy, my understanding is that the accelerometer would only activate at +4.2Gs or -1.8Gs. If an accelerometer activated above 5.4Gs, the airplane had to be thoroughly inspected for structural damage. It really was a turbulent ride. So, in my thoughts, I added that titbit of information to the equation of what I had just been through.

After I completed my paperwork and left the operations center, I headed over to another pilot's room to talk about what happened. When he opened the door and looked at me, his first words were: "What did you do?" As I told him my story, he handed me a beer and calmed my fears about both my decisions and my abilities. I was never reproached for returning to base early and consider myself better lucky than good with regard to the outcome of that day's events. I gained a healthy appreciation and respect for weather and not trusting your equipment too much. And, I had a deeper understanding of the phrase: "It's better to be on the ground wishing you were in the air than to be in the air wishing you were on the ground."

CPT Steve Koenig, 1994

CASTOR 07

Flying a Mohawk for almost a year and a half in Korea, I thought that I had seen it all: bad weather, alerts, last minute changes, preflighting three planes to get one off the ground and of course inflight emergencies. I never really had to handle anything too serious, but in a Mohawk, you didn't expect anything too serious as these were tried and true flying machines. When strapping one on, nothing really worried me and nothing really surprised me. The confidence we had was captured in the phrase: "Flying on freedom's frontier." So, pulling a late night mission wasn't a big deal. The weather forecast was for a beautiful night and a million miles of visibility. I'd have stars to look at, the DMZ fence lit up bright enough to see and it would be calm from one side of the peninsula to the other. If we could take off on time, I'd be home for breakfast, get a few hours work in then call it a day.

OV-1D Mission airplane preparing for departure

I met my Technical Observer (T.O.) and once the mission briefing was completed it was time to preflight and go. The first airplane passed preflight, so we climbed in, strapped in and started the engines. It was going to be a good night.

Off we went on time and on our way. The moon was plenty bright, and we could easily make out both Incheon and Seoul in the distance. Seoul approach frequency was quiet as the only ones flying on the entire peninsula were military and most were inside the military controlled tactical zone. A quick check in with Seoul and we were given our clearance for the night. Climb up to mission altitude, turn away from Seoul and head towards the east coast. The airplane was working fine, things were quiet on the ground and it was more like sightseeing than working tonight. The first trip down the route was almost relaxing. At the east coast, turn around and head back west. I was having fun tonight, in awe of the technology, of the view and of the opportunity to do this type of flying.

Coming up on the lights of Seoul for the second or third time that flight, the radar warning indicator started flickering with a single recurring "lightning bolt" from the north. While not a normal activity, it was known to happen from time to time. "I guess the North Koreans think we're getting sleepy." I mentioned to the TO. He gave me a nod and responded sarcastically: "I hope they don't shoot us down tonight." We both had a laugh and continued on.

However, the radar warning indicator would not quiet down, so we discussed whether it was a real radar threat or a malfunction. The radar warning indicator, like the airplane was vintage Vietnam era equipment, so we dismissed the issue. Time to switch the fuel tanks to make sure we had a balanced load. Another trip on the route completed, reverse course and head back down the route for another trip.

Radar Warning Indicator

With Seoul once again behind us, both the T.O. and I were beginning to relax again when there was a bright flash from the tail and a sudden darkness within the plane. I was looking at the radar warning indicator to see if it showed activity that I somehow missed. The T.O. was screaming but I could hardly hear him as it appeared that the intercom had failed.

I wasn't relaxing any longer. I was wide awake with adrenalin flowing and had a surreal thought: "They shot a f'n a missile at us!" As I scanned the instruments and tried to piece together a coherent and complete picture of what was happening, I had one calming thought: we were still in one piece. The airplane is flying, both engines are working, and the propellers are still turning. With that thought firmly in my mind, the panic subsided. I realized that all the mission equipment was off and the T.O.'s side of the cockpit was completely dark. I had heard from more experienced Mohawk pilots about equipment failures like this, but never expected it would happen to me. With my heart rate and breathing returning to normal, I concluded that an electrical component in the tail of the aircraft had failed, but I still hadn't figured out what the bright flash was. Mohawks did not have any type of fire sensors in the tail so there was no way of telling if a fire had started or the equipment had just shorted out. As I was considering all the possibilities, the T.O. handed me a note which read: "Inverter failure." The mission was over and it was time to head home.

Happy that we were in one piece, I began the coordination process to fly home from my present position. The military controller acknowledged our request, asked if I wanted to divert to a closer airfield or head home. Thanks to the darkness enveloping us, I didn't see any flicker in the tail that would indicate a fire, so I told the controller, we would just head home. He cleared us direct and out of the tactical zone, told us he'd keep an eye on us, then had me switch to Seoul Approach.

This time of the morning, Seoul was a challenge to get a hold of on the radio at best. At times the military controllers called them on the telephone to wake them up so that they would answer their radio. Tonight seemed to be going downhill as we could not reach Seoul on the radio. I called back our military controller and asked him to contact Seoul. After a couple minutes, he came back on and told me he couldn't reach them either but that he would provide flight following to get us home. As our base came into the distance, I told the controller I was visual, so he handed me off to Osan Controllers for the approach.

It's not a bomb, it's a wing tank and it always needed constant fuel balancing

I started running my checklist and was happy to be getting my sick airplane home. As I checked my fuel status, I let out another curse. In all the excitement, I had failed to keep the fuel balanced in both wing tanks and now had to deal with an asymmetric fuel imbalance. I was kicking myself for not maintaining situational awareness but was also happy I caught it at altitude. Unchecked, the imbalance could have caused us to cartwheel on landing as the heavy wing and full fuel tank would have very likely struck the ground and resulted in a loss of control and subsequent crash.

I notified Osan approach of the new problem and requested to hold at altitude until my fuel imbalance could be corrected. I tapped the T.O. on the shoulder and pointed at the fuel gages. He gave me a nod and passed me another note: "How long to burn off the gas?" I estimated a 30 minute hold and wrote it on the paper. He looked at me, shrugged his shoulders and went back to looking out the window As he had nothing to do but look out the window, I'm sure was ready for the night to be over too.

To help burn the fuel quicker, I lowered the landing gear, applied full flaps, set the propellers to max and flew the hold in a standard training maneuver known as slow flight. Although we were flying closer to the stall speed of the aircraft, the configuration would allow us to burn gas at a higher rate thus consuming fuel faster than normal and getting us into a safe, balanced fuel situation to land. The biggest problem with doing this over the airfield, even at our altitude, was that the Mohawks were exceptionally loud. Every Mohawk pilot I knew wore earplugs in addition to the hearing protection the helmet offered because the plane was just that loud. I was sure there were probably a few pilots on the ground wondering what I was doing. Of course, at this point, I didn't care what anybody would think. I was just trying to get home safely. Taking the time to run the checklist might just have saved me from some real embarrassment had I tried to land with a fuel imbalance.

The minutes ticked by and the fuel balanced itself out. I landed without any further incident. After a brief taxied, I shut the engines down and did my walk around. I could see a long black carbon streak on the tail going back from the vent about two feet. I made note of it, handed the crew chief the logbook with the write up: "Suspect inverter failure. Mission equipment inop." I did my debrief, turned in my equipment and headed over to the dining facility for some coffee and breakfast.

I decided to go back over to the hanger after breakfast and check on the airplane. The mechanics had already taken out the inverter. Instead of finding a cube shaped box, I was looking at the distorted inverter. Part of the top was pushed out, it was no longer a cube and showed significant damage. I don't think that it exploded but the damage to the inverter suggested a violent end. One of the mechanics saw me looking at what was left of the inverter and let me know that it had in fact started on fire before it met its final demise. The smoke streak on the side of the plane's tail that I saw on post flight most definitely attested to the fire.

Example of the Inverter component

Why the inverter failed so violently and why the fire did not spread was a mystery. I counted my blessings that morning. Even though I had compounded the initial problem with a fuel imbalance, Grumman Ironworks had safely brought me home.

".... WELL, YOU WRITE IT UP THEN... I'M GETTIN' TH' HELL OUTA HERE..."

HAWK 30

Starting my second year of flying Mohawks in Korea, I was given a new ground job to fill all of my free time (Saying that with all the sarcasm I can muster.). I was assigned as the Battalion Logistician or S4. I was not happy about the job as it was 1996 and the Mohawks were going away. The Army decided they were too old and too expensive to maintain. In Korea, the Air Force was supposed to take over our mission with JSTARS, the darling of Desert Storm and the infamous highway of death. Our airplanes, once they were demilitarized and gutted, would become gunnery targets for the Air Force on the peninsula at Kuni Range. I was the guy responsible for making sure the airplanes were removed from service and put on that range. A horrible job and inglorious end to a real warbird and historic airplane.

As pilots, we knew that our aerobatic, ejection seat "fighter" days were numbered. So, when you were assigned a trainer airplane that didn't have all the mission equipment on it and were told to take it out and practice all your maneuvers, you did just that. Of course, since it could do +6Gs and -3Gs, had inverted fuel tanks and plenty of power, there weren't many aerobatic maneuvers that it couldn't handle. And if you lost control, you could always eject. With the end of an era nearing and the fact that the Army was going to make them gunnery targets, you could say that the training flights, speaking for myself, became aggressive. I found out that a Mohawk would do a nice wing over, terrible tail slide and I could never get it to fly a knife edge very well or for very long. Then there was slow flight. I never really like slowing an airplane down but knew that it was great coordination practice so did it but not as often as I probably should have.

All our training flights were conducted in an area about thirty miles south of Camp Humphreys known as Test Flight Valley. Like the name, the practice area had a very defined east-west ridge line both to the north and to the south with a valley that was about 10 miles wide (or so I remember). There were no towns or villages and not many roads or power lines to deal with in the practice area, so you could fly at tree top level or VFR all the way up to 17,500 feet just like in the states. With only one or two airplanes at a time in Test Flight Valley, it was the ideal place to really have a good time in a Mohawk.

About once a week you could get a trainer if you weren't on the mission schedule. Since I was a primary staff officer, my schedule was never like the company assigned pilots, so I could set up my own schedule as long as I was doing my share of the mission flying. Once in a while, I'd get a call from the scheduling officer asking if I could take a flight. On this beautiful spring day, I was offered a trainer airplane. It was an opportunity to get out of the office and I jumped at the chance to fly.

Initiating a Split-S maneuver

I had just had my assigned training airplane flight a couple days earlier, so I briefed the T.O. that I would be doing some aerobatics but wanted to try some slow flight and power on and off stalls. The T.O.'s response was a "whatever" shrug. We left the briefing to preflight and fly. I headed straight to Test Flight Valley doing a couple aileron rolls along the way. Once in Test Flight Valley, we did a little more with loops and rolls. We flew straight and level for a little bit as most T.O.s didn't handle aerobatics for much more than 15 to 20-minute intervals or they would become nauseous. We had already been at it for about forty-five minutes, so I climbed to 17,500 feet and set up for the power on and power off stalls. For some reason, I remember flying a Cessna 182 in a power off stall configuration and having the instructor show me that with practice, you could "fly the stall" and the airplane would descend in a controlled manner. To do something different, as the Mohawk reached the stall buffett, I thought: "I wonder if a Mohawk would act the same way as the Cessna?"

15th Military Intelligence Mohawk configured for slow
flight "Dirty" flaps and gear extended

At first, I thought it would act in the very same manner, I mean an airplane is an airplane, right? But the Mohawk was not just another airplane. Initially, we did start to descend just like in the Cessna. The stall horn was going off and the stall buffett was strong, but I didn't think it was anything to worry about. The T.O. was more alert but had not asked me anything about what I was doing, so I kept on "flying the stall." The plane continued to descend but was now shaking and the buffett was much stronger, so I was working a little harder than in the Cessna. I was still in control or so I thought. I was thinking to myself; "I've had enough of this shit" and that's when my Mohawk let me know that she wasn't like any other airplane. At that very moment and without any other indications, the plane not only stalled but rolled over and entered a spin, all within a split second. As I struggled to regain control, my training kicked in on spin recovery. The plane continued to spin at an incredible rate of descent, and I also had to deal with the uncomfortable sensation of zero Gs. Being semi weightless in the seat, it was a bit of a challenge pushing opposite rudder. Since I now knew she wasn't a Cessna, I began to wonder if the recovery procedure we were taught in spin training would work. I couldn't remember any other specific recovery training, so just kept the opposite rudder pushed all the way to the stop. Nothing. We were inverted in a spin. I was now a test pilot. I was starting to get a little nervous and conscience of the thoughts of calling for us to eject. Even with full opposite rudder, the plane continued to spin and descend with the vertical speed indicator pegged at 6000 feet per minute. The T.O. was announcing the altitude we were passing all too fast:

"15,000!"

The plane would not stop spinning.

"14,000!"

I remember seeing a Korean hut in the windscreen as I was spiraling down.

"13,000!"

The hut was spinning and getting larger and larger as we were descending.

"12,000!"

I had applied the spin recovery technique as trained, and nothing was happening.

"11,000!"

I was out of ideas as the altitude indicator continued winding down. As we approached 10,000 feet, I was about to command "eject." As if reading my mind, the plane stopped spinning as quickly and suddenly as it had begun. Once the spin stopped, I was able to level the plane and resume normal flight. We were at 8500 feet. I looked at the T.O. and he looked at me. We said nothing.

Although we had only flown for an hour, I decided to cut the flight short. I had had enough for the day. I turned towards Cp Humphreys and descended lower, under control and in silence, flying all the way back to the airfield without a word.

Once I had the airplane shut down and logbook filled out, I sat there thinking about what had happened. I didn't do anything that I could recall except for the recovery technique to stop the spin. Why it seemed to take so long for the plane to recover is beyond me. Before releasing the T.O., I apologized for not briefing him on the maneuver and swore him to secrecy. I promised him unlimited beer anytime I saw him in the clubs outside base. His only comment was: "Let's not do that again."

In post flighting the airplane I paid particular attention to the accelerometers. We had not exceeded any limit despite what it felt like. I would not say anything to anyone. My little secret. I turned in the logbooks mentioning that I returned early to prepare for a staff meeting and headed back to my office.

3rd Military Intelligence Battalion S4, Hawk 30, CPT Steve Koenig, 1996

That evening, the Mohawk company commander came by my room and asked how my flight went. He and I were good friends and I knew he knew something. I fessed up to the spin and told him everything leading up to it. Like me, he didn't have years of experience in Mohawks. As a matter of fact, he was the last graduate of the Mohawk qualification course at Ft. Rucker and Ft. Huachuca before they were both closed. He truly was the last Mohican. He laughed and told me the T.O. had mentioned it to him in the company. He gave me a pass on the incident and told me it wasn't going to be talked about any further. The commander did tell me that he wasn't aware of any other instance where an OV-1 had been spun and successfully recovered. At that point, I handed him a beer and told him he needed to catch up. I was on my third working on a six pack.

I never heard another word and the Battalion Commander never got wind of it. To this day, I think I was lucky more than I was good, but either way, I was alive and learned that "flying the stall" was only something to try in a Cessna.

" ... DID YOU SEE TH' LOOK ON THAT GUY'S FACE ...

VIGILANT 6

Airborne Reconnaissance Low (ARL) de Havilland DHC-7

The Airborne Reconnaissance Low (ARL) program is built on a de Havilland DHC-7 airframe, popularly known as the Dash 7. The four-engine turboprop is loved by its aircrews for its Short Take-Off and Land (STOL) capabilities. The Army uses them globally to supports a number of diverse operations. Originally designed for the 1980's Reagan era drug war in South America, the Dash 7 has been the subject of farfetched articles during its support to the DC Sniper Task Force in 2002 (Newsweek), budget battles over costs to support the largest fleet of Dash 7s in the world, and struggles by different commanders for control and use of the fleet. It is the uniqueness and sophistication of its intel sensors and endurance that make it the jewel in the Army's airborne intelligence fleet. Given its capabilities and responsiveness, it wasn't a surprise when the deployment order arrived in the fall of 2006. The Dash 7 was going to its first real shooting war in Iraq.

Thanksgiving Day 2006 departure

The adventure began with some modifications to sensors and the plane's defensive capabilities. Once complete, we started the deployment. We really didn't think we had much to be thankful for on our departure, Thanksgiving Day, 2006. But, being Soldiers, we sucked it up and began our task.

Our Deployment Flight Route

The flight to Iraq was exciting as we had never done an Atlantic crossing or flown in Europe but also was uneventful. Our route took us up to Canada. We crossed the Atlantic by way of Portugal. Another day into Spain. Then it was onto Italy and then one hop into Turkey. In Turkey, the crew got to stay in VIP quarters. The irony was not lost on me that our last night of peace was in the best quarters available and that the next day we would be in someplace far less lavish. Did someone know more than we did?

To fly from Turkey to Iraq took a lot of coordination and our take off was delayed and then delayed again. Our plan was to arrive in daylight, but close to sunset so as to not be as noticeable a target on landing. We were going to use all the capabilities of the aircraft and make a full STOL landing from 10,000 ft. The strategy was that instead of descending in a standard decent and approach profile of between 10 degrees to 3 degrees, we would be coming down at an almost 45-degree angle or better. We would be a much harder target than a normal approach and landing permits. And, as we trained to do this maneuver it was not going to be overly difficult or challenging. But as the day wore on, we started to realize that we might not make it until after dark and that posed a whole different set of problems.

Vigilant 6 on the ramp in Turkey

First, for safety and security, the runway lights were turned off unless they were requested to be on. If they turned the lights on at night, they were only turned on at the lowest setting and for the briefest amount of time to minimize the risk of rocket or small arms attacks on the plane or the airfield. This was not a problem for most helicopters and tactical aircraft because they were equipped and trained to use Night Vision Goggles (NVGs) or other low light tactical optics. But our aircraft was not equipped for tactical black out operations and we did not train with NVGs. One strike against us.

Second, the airfield we were using was not actually listed in our aviation data base. We had received the longitude and latitude coordinates for the base, not the runway. We were planning on being able to see the runway and line up with it for the landing because it would be daylight. Not anymore. Looking for a black hole on a dark night wasn't something I wanted to do. Strike two.

Lastly, 50,000lb airliners typically turn on a whole bunch of lights when operating in the dark and particularly when landing. It is a safety procedure to be seen and see others, so at night you light yourself up to comply. This rule isn't particularly helpful if you want to stay alive when someone is shooting at you. What you want is to be invisible with the minimal lighting necessary to reduce the probability of becoming a target and increase the probability you can keep breathing. The Dash 7 is large, loud and not too maneuverable so we definitely didn't need to have "Please shoot us down" lights on to make the task any easier. Strike Three.

Being Soldiers and professionals, we had a requirement and a window to fly into Iraq. Delay could cost a day but in reality, a delay might cost American blood. We did not want to risk delaying our arrival or disappointing the task force that was counting on us.

Our take off moved further into the afternoon and the reality of a nighttime arrive was becoming more evident with every passing minute. We requested and received very precise coordinates for each end of the runway. This information allowed us to plan our descent right to the end of the runway and take the guess work out of having to actually look for and find the runway. Next we were able to send a message to the airfield operations office to advise them of the Dash 7's limitations, the need for some runway lighting, and to make sure our approach would be clear of any low flying helicopters or Unmanned Aerial Vehicles (UAVs). Lastly, we spent the hours talking through how we would follow the daylight landing procedures and the changes we would make to land safely in the dark. The plan we came up with was simple, we would fly the approach like we were in the clouds and follow the instruments. We would keep all the lights off until the Radar Altimeter indicated 50ft above the ground. At that point we would turn on just the landing lights and either begin the flare to land or start a go-around to abort the landing.

It was a risky and untired procedure. At 50ft, we would not have a lot of time or altitude to initiate the go-around if we didn't see the runway. But given our circumstances and the desire to get our plane into the fight, we decided it was the best we could do without delaying our arrival.

With our plan made and the airplane finally ready, we left Turkey under the setting sun for the final leg into Iraq. When we crossed the border and checked in with the first of several tactical controllers, the first thing we noticed was that the frequencies were mostly quiet, something I had never experienced in my flying career. The next thing we noticed as darkness blanketed the land was that the country was very dark because the electrical grid was still in disarray and being rebuilt. You could see some smoke and fires in various locations and the sensor operators in the back of the plane were letting us know if they spotted any firefights or other tactical activity. As the half-moon rose, all was quiet and the four turboprops were purring in unison, an most comforting and hypnotizing melody. The initial anxiety and jitters of flying over a real war zone were wearing off. But we had several more hours to go.

All our external lights, strobes and red beacon were all off. We were invisible to the eye. We wanted to be a ghost as much as possible to anyone looking up from the ground. Four turboprops were making plenty of noise, but it's difficult to spot our aircraft day or night, as we were well aware from the other places in the world we operated. So even though you could hear us, you really couldn't see us. Up front, we continued to rehearse what we were going to do, the call outs we would be making and the switches we would be flipping.

The Flight Management Computer (FMC) told us we were approximately 30 minutes away from our new home. We told the tactical controller we were ready to descend to 10,000ft for our final segment of the flight. At 10,000ft, he switched us over to the airfield tower controller.

We properly authenticated and checked-in with the tower. The controllers began to choreograph our arrival with all the NVG and UAV aircraft in the vicinity of the airfield. Short, code word announcements were transmitted and we knew that aircraft were replying and complying with the instructions. As we approached our decent point, we configured the aircraft for a STOL landing, stowed all the sensors and made sure everyone was securely strapped in.

With flaps set to 45 degrees, the gear down, and props set to maximum, the Dash 7 nosed down like a roller coaster going over the top of the first and steepest hill of an amusement park ride and we had the front row seat. In the clear black night, it felt like we were flying straight down towards the ground. It was also very uncomfortable not having any visual cues to aid us in our descent. The runway and taxiways were just one big black hole. We could see buildings with lights, but the actual runway and taxiways were pitch black. So unlike a roller coaster, we couldn't see a thing. We were flying using only FMC information, airspeed, and altimeter to a point we were told was the end of the runway. Without references, in the dark, visual illusions were also playing tricks with us and demanded all our concentration, skill and luck shooting this "blind" approach.

With 5000 feet to go, tower cleared us to land and were standing by to turn on the lights but only at the lowest setting. I notice that we were starting to overfly our runway end point so told the flying pilot to keep the nose down. He replied that we would over speed the flaps if he kept the nose down. I told him better that than miss the runway, land long or have to make a go around in a combat zone. The nose went a little further down.

At 1000 feet I called tower for landing one last time and was told clear to land. At 100 feet I requested the runway lights be turned on. By the time I completed that call, the Radar Altimeter illuminated its 50 foot annunciation. I couldn't see any runway lights and thought: "F __ __ K! We missed it!" But I followed procedure and put on the landing lights. With the flick of the landing light switch, I saw one of the most beautiful sights imaginable, the concrete runway and we were right on centerline. Unfortunately, we still had not touched down as we passed the 4000 feet remaining sign. We settled onto the runway around the 3000-foot marker, feeling a sense of relief. Slowing the plane down, we turned off the landing lights but left our taxi light and navigation lights on. We came to a stop at the end of the runway, turned our only light off with the runway lights going off at almost the same time. In the darkness, we were met by a Soldier with a set of green glowing "chem" sticks to guide us to parking. We shut down a little after midnight.

It was a seven-day journey to Iraq and like many other adventures in flying it was hours of boredom with seconds of terror. The blackness of the night approach, steep descent angle and uncertainty of where or if we would make the runway were only the opening pages in the Dash 7's history supporting operations in Iraq. The following morning, the unit ran its first combat sortie. Since that day, the Dash 7 has continued to serve with distinction in all combat theaters

Vigilant 6 with members of his Battalion on day one in Iraq

LTC Steve Koenig, Vigilant 6, 2005-2007

ALOMA 6

"**H**ey! We're being intercepted!" Screamed the other pilot over the intercom. And as I turned my head to look, a Honduran F-5 fighter came along side with his gear and flaps extended, rocking his wings as he flew along side us. Then he pushed on his afterburner to come around for another pass. It had been ten years since our unit last flew in Honduras. No one had ever heard of our airplanes being intercepted anywhere we flew because we were invited to fly and had the approval of the host nation to do what we were doing, so this was quite a surprise. Neither I nor the other pilot I was flying with could believe we were being intercepted. We had an approved US / Honduran flight plan. We were flying in Visual Meteorological Conditions (see and be seen) and had been doing our mission for almost an hour. WTF!

Freeze frame photo of the Honduran F-5 intercepting our Dash 7

The F-5 had come back around and pulled into position next to us again for a quick wing rock. (The wing rock is recognized as the international sign that you are being intercepted and you need to follow the intercepting aircraft.) We both realized the F-5 was having trouble flying slow next to our de Havilland "Dash" 7. He was almost stalling his supersonic fighter trying to match our slow airspeed. Let the fun begin......

Freeze frame photo of the Honduran F-5 wing rocking to our Dash 7

We acknowlegded the intercept and follow me signs. But, as we were on an authorized mission, we needed time to shut our systems down and notify our higher authority via radio that we had been intercepted. We also needed to let everyone on our other radio net know what was going on and our intentions to comply with the instructions to land. Lastly, we had to make sure the crew complied with all the regulations pertaining to our systems so that we would be able to let anyone on the ground inspect us if it became necessary. So to make some time for ourselves, we slowed our aircraft down even more to make the F-5's intercept mission that much tougher. I don't think the Honduran Air Force practices much slow flight in the F-5s and we were having a good laugh watching this poor fighter pilot try to slow down without stalling and crashing his airplane.

While enjoying the F-5 pilot's misery, we found a frequency for an airport we had flown by some thirty minutes earlier. It was a dual military / civilian airfield and we guessed that the F-5 had taken off out of that location. We tried contacting the F-5 directly using internationally agreed upon intercept procedures, but he did not respond. So, we contacted the airport control tower. The tower controllers were very happy to hear from us and although we identified ourselves and requested they contact the Honduran military, they informed us that we needed to land, "Or Else." Although the threat was somewhat unpleasant, the F-5 had no weapons that we could see and we had international markings of an American registered airplane, so we didn't think they were serious. But, we knew it best to follow the protocol, so we contacted our own higher authority and made plans to land.

Freeze frame of infrared photo of Honduran F-5 with his afterburner on

OMG! When I called our higher authority and informed them that we had been intercepted, you would have thought I had told them we were on fire and about to crash! I had no idea as to how many different units monitored our net. I must have had 10 different voices trying to contact me for more information about what was happening. The different voices even started arguing with one another over the radio! Pure chaos ensued. When there was a break on the frequency, I politely but firmly informed everyone on the net that I was both the unit commander and the captain of the flight and was not going to provide any more information until I was back on the ground at our base airport. And then I told them I was shutting off the radio. After that exchange, the pilot I was flying with, a senior Warrant Officer, looked at me and with a sheepish smile told me that it was nice knowing me. The implied sarcasm was that he expected me to be relieved or beheaded, I'm not sure which. I told him, I'd deal with the fall out after we were home in the states.

I received confirmation from my crew that the airplane was ready to land at the airport. The air traffic controllers cleared me to land and to "follow the military police jeep to parking". The jeep was equipped with a machine gun which the gunner had trained on us as we followed them to a parking spot. Unlike the weaponless F-5, the machine-gun was loaded and the soldier acted like he knew how to handle the weapon. We parked and shut down the airplane.

The nice thing about what was happening was that our plane had four Spanish speaking Soldiers on board. I told the crew to stay in the plane. I and the most senior Spanish speaking Soldier got out to talk with our reception committee: Several Honduran Air Force officers and more security.

Example of our reception committee upon landing

I and my interpreter saluted the senior officer. With my Soldier translating, we introduced ourselves, explained our flight plan and purpose (training flights) and asked them to check with the Honduran operations center. The Honduran Colonel replied in English, politely thanking us for following the intercept protocol and introducing us to his accompanied staff. He told us that it would take approximately an hour to hear back and that we would have to remain with our aircraft until the situation was sorted out. So, we stood around making small talk and watching the F-5 pilot do low passes and victory rolls over the airfield.

The Colonel explained that F-5 pilots do not receive many actual flight hours and that the intercept pilot had to reduce the F-5's weight for landing by burning off his extra fuel, hence the impromptu air show. Most of us on the Dash 7 believed that the F-5 pilot was probably going to be highly decorated for the "live" intercept and protecting his nation's sovereign borders.

Approximate location of our flight route, intercept and starting point

Sure enough, almost exactly an hour later, the Colonel came up to me to apologize for interfering with our mission. He explained that the Honduran operation center did not forward our flight plan because we were not going to be landing at any airfield and we were operating accordingly to international Visual Flight Rules and outside of any controlled airspace. The Colonel went on to explain that the civilian controllers only notified him of our flight after an approaching commercial airplane noticed us flying along the sea shore and thought we might be drug runners. While it seemed far fetch to think a fifty thousand pound, four engine airplane would be trying to sneak in and transport narcotics, it wasn't impossible. We thanked our host and got ourselves back in the air. Our mission over, we headed home.

Back in the air, it was a short flight to base. The entire flight crew thought it was cool getting intercepted. I was dreading all the phone calls that I would be making to locations throughout the US and South

America. I knew that while the unit and the flight had been conducted correctly and professionally, there would be many questions asked about our training and procedures to have let something like this happen.

Army de Havillian "Dash" 7

You see, arm chair quarterbacking of flight operations is common in the Army where aviation units have higher headquarters that are full of non-rated, ground based officers. So, I took the heat, answered the questions and prepared for the next mission.

Walking out of the base operations center, I was proud of the way the crew handled the situation and actually felt sorry for the Honduran Colonel. A small SNAFU could have caused a large international incident. Everyone was trying to do the right thing and it wasn't the first time an Army airplane was intercepted but it wasn't common either.

After the initial blowback, the unit and I were both commended for our own professionalism and most importantly, I kept my rank, command and my head.

Outside base operations the day after the intercept

ALOMA 6 POSTSCRIPT

At the time of publication I am aware of two other documented friendly nation intercepts. While there are no details, this F-18 intercept happened over Switzerland in the 2000s. And a U-21 was intercepted by Danish F-16s in 1985.

Swiss F/A-18 off the wing of an unknown Army C-12

Danish F-16 off the wing of unknown U-21 in 1985

"... EVERYBODY FREEZE! ... NOBODY MOVE! O'GRADY SAYS CONTROLLER TRAINING IS IN PROGRESS ... "

ARMY 58CL

In February 2006, I was fortunate to ferry one of the Army's de Havilland "Dash" 7s, tail number N158CL, from Hagerstown, MD to South Korea. I and my crew planned the route and after presenting the plan to both the battalion and brigade commanders, received approval for the flight. Our route was new and less conservative than previous Pacific crossings. Our route would allow us to fly from Maryland to Korea in seven days if all went well. The best any previous ferry flights had done was over 14 days. Our route had a higher risk and the only comment we received from the brigade commander was: "If you have an emergency, ditch in the Pacific and wait for rescue. Don't land in Russia." Not a great way to kick off our flight.........

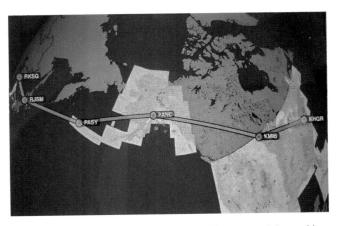

Lots of blue ocean to cross and almost halfway around the world

We flew an uneventful first leg from Hagerstown to Minot AFB, ND except that the heat didn't work. As our departure was in February, temperatures both on the ground and in the air were not conducive to comfort. So, while we were over Ohio, our civilian mechanic told us he could fix the heat while in flight. The mechanic knew what the issue was with the heat and asked us to turn off the bleed air so he could investigate and attempt a repair. The bleed air system controls the air conditioning and heat as well as the pressurization, so turning it off was not something that we wanted to do for too long. We would have to use supplemental, portable oxygen while the system was off so that we would not become hypoxic. We were at 18,000 feet and wanted to continue with the flight. In the cold of the cockpit, the plan sounded reasonable, so we donned our oxygen masks and shut off the bleed air.

Our mechanic bundled up on the leg from Minot to Anchorage

About 20 minutes after turning off the bleed air, we noticed that the mechanic had not made his way back to the cockpit. We looked back and saw our mechanic was in the prone position and not moving. I transferred control of the aircraft to the copilot and went back to check on the mechanic. Overweight and a heavy smoker, the mechanic had taken off his O2 mask while looking under the floorboards of the aircraft. He had passed out due to lack of oxygen! I placed his mask on him, yelled to the flying pilot to turn on the bleed air, and waited for the mechanic to arise from his oxygen deprived stupor. Needless to say, he didn't get the heat fixed either. After a seven hour flight, we arrived in Minot as cold as I ever wanted to be. We stayed on base in Minot and let the mechanic work on the heating system. It was going to be even colder on the next leg to Juneau, Alaska.

Two of the "Four fans of freedom"

When we arrived at the plane the next day, the temperature was 15° Fahrenheit with a wind chill of -14° Fahrenheit. Our mechanic had repaired the heating system overnight and prepped the aircraft for our departure to Juneau. We preflighted in the cold and climbed in to get things warmed up by starting the engines. We attempted to start the number 3 engine to no avail. We then tried starting number 4, then number 2 and finally number 1. The engines were too cold and would not start. The plane had remained outside all night, the fuel was way too cold to ignite; not something we'd thought of as the airplanes were always hangered in Korea and elsewhere. Our mechanic obtained a portable airplane heater from the Air Force and used the heater to warm each engine separately so that they would start. After a longer than normal warm up at idle, we took off late for Juneau.

Once airborne, things began to go our way on this leg. We were flying the Dash -7 with an approved takeoff weight of 50,000 pounds (normal maximum takeoff weight is 47,000 pounds) and the aircraft had a supplemental type certificate (STC) for an auxiliary fuel system. While over the Canadian Rockies, with the extra gas, we determined we could make Anchorage, Alaska instead of Juneau. Landing in Anchorage on this leg would shave off one day of our planned ferry trip.

We coordinated with ATC to change our destination, but they mandated that we climb to 23,000 feet to ensure safe clearance over the Rockies as well as to maintain ATC communications. We complied with the climb but the low, slow, lumbering Dash 7 took over 45 minutes to climb from 18,000 feet to 23,000 feet. And even though the heating system was fixed, the temperature was so cold that we had to bundle up with jackets and gloves and place the engine inlet cover "plugs" under our feet to prevent frostbite. The PT6-50 engines do not produce much horsepower over 15,000 feet so the heating system suffers first.

When we arrived in the Anchorage area, heavy snow and icing was prevalent. However, the aircraft performed exceptionally well and we landed at Anchorage without incident after the eleven hour and twenty minute flight. The next day we explored Anchorage to maintain compliance with "crew rest" regulations. We enjoyed visits to Mary's Diner for pie, and a must for any aviator is a visit to the largest sea plane base in the world, Lake Hood.

The following day, we canceled our departure to Shemya, Alaska due to low ceilings and visibility there. Additionally, just a month earlier a volcano located in Kodiak, Mount Augustine, began erupting and was still belching ash in the area. This concerned us somewhat as volcanic ash can cause erosion of the props and engines. So, we enjoyed the added day in Anchorage and left Anchorage a day late for an eight-and-a-half-hour flight to Shemya. Located 1200 miles from Anchorage, Shemya is a postage stamp of an island at the very end of the Aleutian chain. At the height of the Cold War, it was a 1200 man US Air Force base. Now it's got less than a couple hundred residents. We were met by the local personnel who made us feel welcome (Said sarcastically as the welcome sign attests to.). The highlight of being in Shemya is the encounters with blue foxes. They will come up to you and beg for food and follow you around until you give them something to eat.

Out in the cold. Not something the Dash 7 is used to.

The Army wasn't special enough to receive a personal welcome at Shemya

The next leg was probably our most challenging and I had our brigade commander's guidance not to land in Russia echoing in my ears. We were flying over the Pacific Ocean all the way from Shemya to Misawa, Japan. Our only options for any emergencies were to return to Shemya or make it to Japan. While we trusted our aircraft and our maintenance, you have to consider that we were flying a plane built in the early 1970s and maintained by the lowest bidder. The morning of departure, our weather briefing showed favorable winds for the trip and good weather. We took-off for our oceanic leg and left land behind.

Roughly an hour after departure we met with headwinds much stronger than our forecast. The Air Data Computer was showing winds between 40-105 knots. We had a "go/no go" decision point planned for our flight and with some trepidation, continued our flight to the go/no go point four hours into the flight in the hope of the winds changing (as forecasted). Three hours into the flight and with an hour to go to the go/no go point, the copilot let me know that the fuel calculations were not looking good. He was getting nervous and so was I but not enough to turn back just yet. I told him we needed to stick with the plan and fly for another hour. After about ten minutes of silence, my copilot turned to me and stated that I was in a state of denial. "We don't have the fuel to make it to Misawa." He nervously but confidently stated. I calmly replied that we only had another 45 minutes to go before reaching the go/no go point. The copilot acquiesced and began recalculating the fuel numbers for the fourth or fifth time. With ten minutes to the go/ no go point, we cleared the weather and the headwind lessened to less than 30 knots. Our fuel consumption went from ditching in the Pacific to having our reserve fuel available.

Beautiful blue sky ahead after breaking out of the weather just prior to the go/no go point

While we were both still nervous, the winds were forecast as a tail wind pushing us the rest of our flight. Based on the total fuel onboard we made the decision to continue to Misawa. After ten hours over the Pacific, Japan came into view and we landed in Misawa at 4pm local. This leg was eleven and half hours in flight, a new record set for the Dash 7. We took off at 50,000 lbs and flew over 2250 air miles at a block altitude between 10,000-16,000 feet to search for best wind conditions. We encountered light icing conditions and light turbulence during the flight. We had 17,576 lbs of fuel at takeoff and landed with 1076 lbs on board. The feeling of satisfaction and relief we felt cannot be overstated.

Upon arrival in Misawa, we asked if they could put the aircraft in the hangar but there was no space available. We were once again parked on the freezing cold ramp. We asked about the possibility of snow overnight and were told that it was not in the forecast. Of course, the next day we woke up to two feet of new snow. We called dispatch and asked them for a deicing truck. Once the truck arrived, it took over two hours to remove all the snow and ice from the aircraft.

We departed Misawa and flew the shortest leg of the flight, arriving at Osan Air Base, South Korea to clear customs then a quick hop to Camp Humphreys. When we shut the engines down at 6pm local, our trip had taken 43.8 hours, six landings and seven days. It was one of the fastest ferry flights from the USA to Korea for a Dash 7. Twenty-four hours later, the airplane was back flying the "Frontiers of Freedom" as it had been doing for over twenty years and continues to do so to the current day.

Army 58CL

GRIZZLY 22

M ost flights in a de Havilland Dash 7 are hours of boredom for the pilots with hours of intense surveillance for the sensor operators in the back of the airplane. Even in a war zone the mission can become routine, even casual. For the troops on the ground, we're the eyes and ears of the battlefield, the all seeing all knowing voice on the radio that lets them know when it's safe and when danger is a foot. By the time the unit had completed our first 1000 hours in Iraq, we had become an integral piece of every mission for the elite units we supported. They trusted us and we knew we were making a difference.

Grizzly 22 Detachment in Iraq, Spring 2007

They say that routine and repetition are good in large aircraft operations, but in the Spring of 2007, in Iraq, supporting combat operations, one routine mission turned into one of those stories that validates the saying that truth is stranger than fiction.

Like all days and all missions in Iraq, the day starts off early. In the hot, dusty and dry waking hours, there is a briefing with the troops on the ground prior to departure, a flight crew briefing, and of course checks and inspections that everyone has a functional weapon, combat gear, snacks and drinks, communications frequencies and of course the target set. It's a little more than just kicking the tires, lighting the fire and briefing on Guard as the old timers might think.

Up in the air and on our way, the first danger is behind us, getting above small arms range. Now it's out to the target area to establish our loiter and collect our intel. For the pilots up front we can have our first cup of coffee, get up and use the lavatory and settle in for what will be another long day in the air. The air conditioning is working great, our troops on the ground are happy with what we're doing, all is well.

Grizzly 22 off on another combat mission

After about an hour and a half and too many cups of coffee, it's time to "walk to the back", as we say, to use the lavatory. I let the other pilot go first and keep an eye on the plane: Systems normal, dusty brown outside, happy customers. As the copilot comes back, he seemed a little distracted, so I ask what's the matter? He tells me that as he was talking to the sensor operators, one of them, a Sergeant, has the non-verbal signal for distress on his workstation. The copilot made eye contact with the operator and when he did, he gestured ever so slightly to the other operator. The copilot acknowledged that he understood and then made his way forward to the flight deck. I couldn't imagine why the sensor operator would use the distress signal as everything was going well and "we," Grizzly 22, were not under any distress.

The copilot and I discussed the situation and agreed that we needed to talk to the Sergeant without alerting the other sensor operator, a Private First Class (PFC). We called the Sergeant on the intercom to come up to the flight deck and re-load our encrypted radio because it wasn't working properly. As crypto loads and codes were one of the Sergeant's normal duties, we knew that he could come up and talk to us away from the PFC. He was on the flight deck within a minute of our request, just like normal.

When he got between us, he told us in a very hurried and tense voice that the PFC had pulled his M16A2 rifle, chambered a 5.56mm round and pointed it at the Sergeant. He then told the Sergeant that he was deciding whether or not to kill him. He held the rifle on the Sergeant until he saw the copilot leave the flight deck to use the lav. He had placed the rifle on his work station, still pointing it at the Sergeant with his finger on the trigger and the safety off. We told the Sergeant to go back to his workstation and get back to work while we discussed the safest way to diffuse the situation, secure the PFC's weapon and transition the mission to another aircraft. Yep, the Sergeant had used the distress signal correctly and we had a very real and dangerous situation on our hands.

The fact that this PFC had done this was quite surprising and shocking for a number of reasons. First, this PFC was experienced and senior enough that he had been handpicked to be one of the few sensor operators to deploy with the initial detachment. Second, the PFC was up for promotion to Corporal and had been recommended for promotion by the entire chain of command. Third, he and the

Sergeant he was flying with this day were friends on the ground and considered "battle buddies" or mostly best friends. They lived in the trailer on the Forward Operating Base and were inseparable on the ground both here and back at our home base. Lastly, the PFC only the week before been awarded an impact Air Medal for identifying an ambush and giving the ground force sufficient time and information to both avoid the ambush and surround and capture/kill the would be ambushers. Not exactly the kind of Soldier you would expect to lose it on the battlefield.

Typical M16A2

We also had to consider the possibility that the PFC had had some sort of news from home that caused him to do what he did. Unlike previous conflicts in previous times, every Soldier in Iraq had access to both the internet and a cell phone. It wasn't surprising to have a Soldier call home during a rocket attack or just after some an intense operation while the adrenaline was still flowing. I recall hurriedly finishing a conversation with my wife with the comment: "there's a rocket attack going on. I gotta get my gear on." When I called her back the next evening, while she was relieved, she also let me know that I didn't need to tell her everything that was going on.

Given that the PFC had chambered rounds and his weapon was hot, we needed to consider him a threat not only to the Sergeant, but to all of us crewing the mission. We had a real situation that could conceivably cause the death of everyone on board the airplane as well as the loss of a one of a kind airplane. The PFC had the potential to kill us all and crash the airplane if he wanted. Was he suicidal, homicidal, crazy or bluffing? We needed to get control of his weapon and him, and we needed to do it without him deciding to open fire on us first.

Luck was on my side that day as my copilot had previously been a Special Forces Sergeant First Class. He understood the situation, had experience dealing with Soldiers in crisis and was a specimen of physical fitness. While not a tall or large man, he had the physical strength to win a wrestling contest and the training to win a fight, if it came to it. He volunteered to go back and get the weapon and subdue the PFC. The plan was simple and straight forward. The copilot would go back and use the lav. When he was done with the lav, he would go over to the PFC's workstation and ask him how the mission was going. He would lean over the workstation, rest one hand on the barrel of the rifle and one hand on the PFC's shoulder. This would give him the leverage necessary to move the rifle barrel off the Sergeant, and should a struggle ensue, give him position over the seated PFC. Best of all, he would be behind the PFC and could easily put him in a choke hold if necessary. My part of the plan was to give a mission change to the operators and then do the in-flight mission briefing over the intercom to further distract the PFC.

At this point, we were ready with the plan, but you have to wonder why the other sensor operators didn't notice what was going on. The answer is that because of the arrangement of the workstations and the differences in the equipment being used. The other sensor operators were in front of the Sergeant and PFC and worked facing forward, like in a classroom. They were involved with their own responsibilities supporting the mission so would not look backward (unless they were getting up to use the lav). As a result of the configuration and focus on their responsibilities, the PFC could keep his eyes on everyone else's movements. It was only the Sergeant across the aisle in his workstation that could see the PFC. Additionally, the intercom for the operators could be configured so that the adjacent workstations could talk to each other privately without interfering with anyone else's communications. In intel speak, the airplane was designed for compartmentalization: Each workstation was a world of its own, well almost.

Example of compartmented workstation

With the copilot ready, I wished him luck and got busy giving the operators the fake mission change. I then began the in-flight mission briefing. My only clue of success or failure in the situation in the back was going to either be shots fired or the copilot walking back to the flight deck with an M16.

For me, alone on the flight deck, it was a long, anxious couple minutes. I never in my career envisioned a Soldier trying to kill another Soldier inside of one of our airplanes. And the only thing I could do if he started firing, would be to put the airplane into a hard bank and aggressive dive to throw the attacker off balance and attempt an emergency off airport landing. I did not relish landing a turboprop airliner in the desert of Iraq and the probability of walking away unscathed was not very promising.

I completed the mission briefs and then switched off the intercom to the operators. Although my copilot had not returned, all was quiet in the back, for the moment at least. With the mission briefing done, I began the coordination process to abort the mission and conduct a relief on station with another aircraft. I told the tactical operation center that I had a maintenance issue and would update them on the ground. Although it didn't happen often, there was no fuss or challenge as it wasn't the first time we had a maintenance issue and couldn't complete the mission. I broke station and started the flight home. But for the operators in back, the maneuvering was all a part of flying to a new location per the fake mission brief.

I was starting to get nervous. While I heard nothing from the back, voices, gunshots, a fight or the intercom, the copilot should have had the PFC's weapon by now and the situation should have been under control. Was my copilot now just another hostage for the PFC? I had no idea and there was no way to check as I could not see much of anything by looking back from the flight deck. The thoughts that started running through my head were not pleasant. What was going on back there?

I was finishing the turn home and leveling the wings focused on flying. From the corner of my eye, I see an M16 and I think I nearly soiled myself. Recovering quickly, I realized that the copilot was thrusting the M16 through the flight deck entrance in triumph. I turned to look and saw a big smile of relief on his face. My copilot told me that he took the rifle without incident and that the PFC admitted to him that he was thinking of killing the Sergeant. When asked why, the PFC told the copilot that it was because the Sergeant had been teasing him about his losing sports team. The PFC had asked the Sergeant to stop teasing him but he kept on teasing him. The PFC said it had been going on all week and that he was tired of it, so threatening to kill the Sergeant had finally shut him up.

With the PFC's weapon secured, the PFC was removed from his workstation. The two forward operators were told that the mission was over and what had happened just a few feet behind them. They were then instructed to keep an eye on the PFC until we were on the ground. They were also told that if he tried anything they had permission to beat the living crap out of the PFC.

When we landed we were met by the detachment First Sergeant who took the PFC across the Forward Operating Base to the hospital for a physical and psychological evaluation. His war was over and so was his enlistment in the Army. The only decision was whether to discharge or prosecute. The command we were supporting was as shocked as we were to hear what happened. With their help, the PFC was flown back to our home station and admitted for a full psychological evaluation and recommendation.

In the press and to the public, this is sometimes called a "Green on Green" engagement. As we neither wanted nor needed the exposure because of the sensitivity of our operations, the PFC was prosecuted under the military's justice system and was subsequently given an "Other than Honorable" Discharge. To prosecute and discharge him took almost 45 days. His split decision cost him his career and his future.

For Grizzly 22, it was only one mission of many. But it was probably the most scary and harrowing flights for anyone assigned to our unit flying anywhere in the world. And, as the PFC was never deemed to have any mental disorder, none of us really know why he did what he did on that mission. The fact that he didn't carry out his threat was a great relief to all of us. We lived to fly another day.

"... NOW, THOSE ARE REAL V I P PILOTS..."

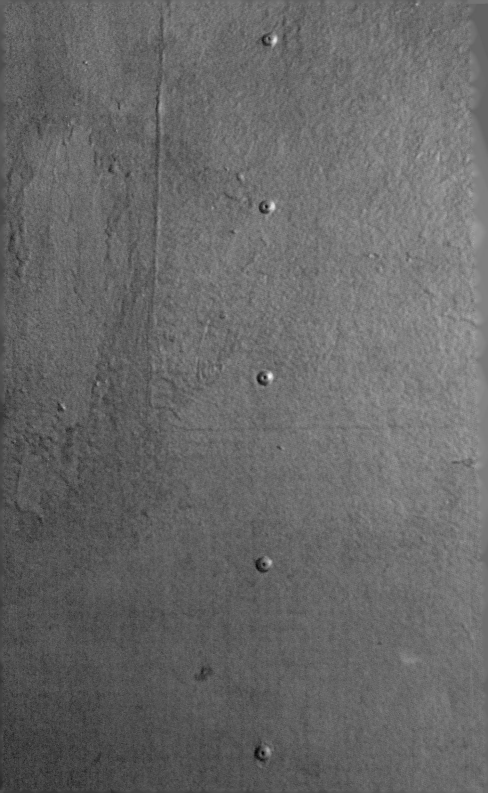

GOLDEN KNIGHT 608

In 2002, I was selected to join the US Army Golden Knights as their Aviation Detachment Commander. The Golden Knights, officially titled the US Army Parachute Team, are one of three Department of Defense sanctioned demonstration teams, the others being the US Navy Blue Angels and the US Air Force Thunderbirds. I was with the Golden Knights for four years, from 2002 to 2006, and participated in a lot of great and memorable missions. However, this one mission was definitely the highlight of my time there.

As an airplane pilot, this assignment was meant to both broaden my flying experience as well as be a reward for a longer than normal tour of duty in Korea. The assignment was outside the conventional career path for an Army Aviation Officer and could also mean that my future for promotion was either not very promising or just the opposite. Depending what day of the week it was, I sometimes thought it meant the former.

It was also a different type of flying than what I was used to. I spent my first four years as an Army pilot flying UH-1H Huey and UH-60A/L Black Hawk helicopters before transitioning into airplanes. My first and previous airplane assignment before joining the Golden Knights involved flying intelligence and reconnaissance aircraft in Korea. The mission profile for these aircraft included a lot of "straight and level" flying and maximum use of the auto-pilot in order to stabilize the aircraft to both facilitate intelligence collection and increase the accuracy of the sensors. Flying for the Golden Knights involved a lot more "stick and rudder" flying and minimal use of the auto-pilot. It was important for the team during training to get in as many jumps as possible to master their complex choreography while free falling as well as safely performing multiple canopy "ladders" and formations. To achieve maximum jumps in a given day, the pilots needed to rapidly execute a lot of take-offs, climbs, descents, and landings. This type of old school "seat of the pants" flying really hones your feel for the aircraft by focusing more outside the aircraft than inside on the instrument panel to let you know what the aircraft is doing.

The Golden Knights pilots are selected by name unlike normal pilot assignments. Most pilots selected to the detachment have thousands of hours of airplane experience and multiple flying assignments under their belts. However, as noted above, the flying is quite different from flying intelligence missions and even more so when compared to flying passengers. You usually spend your first six months or so learning the aircraft by flying local training flights close to the Golden Knights home at Ft. Bragg, North Carolina.

The Golden Knights operate two types of aircraft, the first being the Fokker F-27 Troopship or C-31 as it is formally designated by the Department of Defense. The C-31 is the larger of the two planes and can carry about 50 passengers. It is used primarily to support the team at air shows and other demonstrations.

Fokker F-27 Troopship / C-31

The de Havilland DHC-6 Twin Otter, or Department of Defense designated UV-18, is the other type of aircraft the team operates. It is mainly used for local parachute training support. It is the smaller of the two types, is easier to operate, and is the first aircraft newly assigned pilots are qualified in. After a few months of cutting your teeth on the Twin Otter you begin your C-31 qualification and upon completion of this training you begin touring with the team in support of air shows, sporting events, and on occasion, high-profile demonstrations at the national level. It is the latter that is the beginning of my story.

de Havilland DHC-6 Twin Otter / UV-18

This important chapter of my life spurned a tremendous number of stories for the future grandkids and "there I was" tales for my fellow aviators. However, there was one event during my time there that stands out above the others. Former President George H.W. Bush celebrated his 75th birthday on June 12th, 1999 by skydiving with the Golden Knights. For his 80th birthday he wanted to do a repeat of his 75th and I was fortunate enough to have been a part of the team when the request came in from the Bush family.

For those that don't know, President Bush flew 58 combat missions in TBF Avenger airplanes during WWII, earning the Distinguished Flying Cross and three Air Medals. He made his first parachute jump on September 2, 1944, when the Avenger he was flying got hit by Japanese anti-aircraft fire. So, he was an old hand at jumping out of airplanes by the time I would fly for his jump.

In preparation for his birthday jump, we hosted the former President at Ft. Bragg a few weeks prior to his jump for some free fall training in the wind tunnel. This also provided the Jump Masters with an opportunity to do some classroom refresher training with him prior to the team jumps scheduled at College Station and Houston, Texas. Both locations were hosting celebrations for his upcoming birthday events. As they did with his 75th birthday jump, it was the job of the Golden Knights to make his 80th birthday jump a joyous occasion worthy of celebration.

On June 9th, 2004 we flew one C-31 and one UV-18 to College Station, Texas, which would be our staging area for the President's jumps. The UV-18 was the primary aircraft we would use for the tandem jumps, to include the President's. The C-31 was brought to drop our demonstration team out for a night jump as part of the birthday celebration.

I flew an uneventful flight from Pope Air Force Base to College Station in the C-31 with a refuel stop in Meridian Mississippi. June 10th and 11th, we were guests of the Bush family and were treated to a real Texas barbeque and private tour of the Presidential Library in College Station. The Bush's were true Texans in their hospitality and generous with their time. They made themselves available to the entire team for individual photos, team photos and autographs. It was a tremendous thrill to actually shake hands with the President and have a few minutes to speak with him. Although I honestly don't remember what I said, I do know that I was awestruck to introduce myself to a WWII veteran, hero and genuine American Treasure.

President Bush (41) signing a book for CPT Counts outside his Presidential Library.

On June 12th, in preparation for the demonstration team's jump into Minute Maid Park that night, we repositioned the C-31 from College Station to Houston Hobby airport. We began our pre-flight rituals that included inspecting the aircraft, checking the weather, filing our flight plan, and all the other necessary items that on the surface appear mundane but serve a critical role in the safety of the flight. While we were busy doing our pilot stuff, the crew chief was busy ensuring the aircraft's fluids were topped off and all cargo was battened down. The demonstration team was busy doing final checks of their gear and rehearsals. A team jump during the day was challenging enough but night adds its own set of unique challenges. Toss in the complexities of a stadium, such as Minute Maid Park, and it's like trying to make a basketball shot from half court with one eye closed while moving at ninety miles an hour.

To CPT Kevin Counts
Thanks for your service to our nation — Thanks
for making #41 feel so young. Best always,

CPT Counts in the shadow, second row left of President Bush

The Minute Maid Park event was the main celebration and included numerous celebrities and guest speakers. President George W. Bush (43) flew down for his father's celebration and we had an opportunity to meet him and get a team picture beside Air Force One before he joined his father.

It was now getting close to jump time and we began our final checks, then cranked both Rolls Royce Dart engines. The Golden Knights were scheduled to perform the night jump called the "fireball."

The team would parachute into the stadium with special pyro devices strapped to their ankles to light up the night sky over Houston. The "fireball" is a really great show for the spectators on the ground. But from the air flying the airplane, I had to settle for banking the plane away from the team after they jumped out so I rarely got a view of the display.

We finished our engine run-up and as is procedure I called my boss, the Golden Knights Commander, on my cell phone to see if we were still a go. My commander was sitting next to 41 and 43 inside the stadium. He told me to hold off a bit longer as the guest speakers were going a little longer than planned. With the guest speakers running long, I was concerned that we might violate our FAA jump waiver which was only good for a 90-minute period. While 90-minutes might sound like a lot of time, our wind check, climb, and other pre-jump rituals eat up around 30-45 minutes. It was not unusual to find ourselves jammed up against the backside of the 90-minute waiver window. Because these waivers were usually signed by a very senior FAA official during a standard 9-5, five-day work week, experience had taught us that it wasn't always easy to get them changed on the fly. Although I was a military pilot, I could still lose my FAA certificate if I violated the waiver. So, when things started to go long, I had reason to worry. I was certain that this senior FAA official wasn't going to be readily available on a Saturday night, even with two Presidents waiting for our performance.

The 15-minute delay turned into a 30-minute delay. The exhaust from the Rolls Royce engines was seeping into the aircraft through the open jump doors and mixing with the humid Houston night. I was worried about our waiver time and decided to call the boss back for an update. He said the guest speakers were still way behind schedule and told me to ring up the FAA and get an extension to the waiver. As my boss was sitting next to the "ultimate" waiver authority, I somewhat sarcastically but yet somewhat seriously suggested that he just ask the President to approve an extension. If I could get verbal approval from the President of the United States, I'd be willing to risk my wings and go for it. Unfortunately, my boss did not see either the humor or seriousness that I did and was far from comfortable with asking the President for a verbal approval. In true military fashion, I told him I'd do my best with the FAA and call him back.

Sitting at the controls with the Golden Knights jump team on board, I'm sure the ground controller at Houston Hobby hadn't received any request along the lines of what I was getting ready to send his way. However, I thought the worse that could happen is they'd laugh and tell us to shut down our engines and have a good trip back to the hotel. I swallowed nervously and with the key of the mic button I went for it:

"Houston Hobby Ground this is Golden Knight 608 with a request".

"Golden Knight 608 go ahead with your request".

"Yes sir, we're delayed for our jump into Minute Maid Park tonight and will need a waiver extension from the FAA".

Although I was expecting something along the lines of laughter, a verbal taunt of "ice water in hell" or some other euphemism for not only "no," but "hell no," the controller told me he'd see what he could do.

I knew it wasn't a big secret who we were supporting but, except for me asking my boss to intercede directly with the President, I always played it by the book and didn't ask for any favors. Golden Knight pilots had a great reputation for working with the FAA controllers. The jumps tie up a lot of their airspace, so we try to not come off as prima donnas and want to be considered team players. Much to my surprise and within minutes of the initial call, the controller came back and told us that his boss contacted the FAA approval authority at home, and we had a verbal extension to take all the time we needed to complete the mission. I guess the FAA approval authority knew we were supporting two Presidents too and wanted to keep his job.

I finally got the call to take off almost an hour and ten minutes later than planned. The demonstration team jumped into Minute Maid Stadium much later than we planned but on time as far as the Presidents were concerned. The team lit up the night sky over Houston, Texas and the police even received a few calls as did the UFO Hotline. The stress of flying for two Presidents, needing an extension to perform and a successful jump gave me reason to beam with pride as we shut the airplane down for the night.

The winds on June 13th were outside the limits of man and parachute that morning. However, the same George H.W. Bush that made it out of a crippled TBF Avenger all those years ago during World War II said he was ready to go, winds be damned. I admired his spunk and was ready to roll myself, from the safety of the cockpit of course. However, our Jump Masters stepped in and in coordination with our Commander, Mrs. Bush, and the Secret Service, cooler heads prevailed.

President Bush (41) after his 80th birthday parachute jump

Instead of allowing the President to go solo, it was decided to strap him to one of our Tandem Jump Masters and have him free fall from 13,000 feet with one of our best. President George H.W. Bush made his second successful jump from the UV-18 and I was at the controls. Just like the jump into Minute Maid Park the night before, this jump was another Golden Knights success story.

The Bush family treated us with nothing but dignity and respect. I really felt as if I was visiting with friends instead of a United States President and his family. I was stunned by some of the reporting I saw from the media accusing the Bush family of misutilizing taxpayer funds. The reporting was wrong. The Bush family paid for all our expenses to include the cost of the aircraft and crews. They also paid for all of the President's equipment and even donated it to the Golden Knights Museum at Ft. Bragg.

Looking back, it's hard to believe this event occurred over 14 years ago. In those same 14 years I have deployed three times, flown hundreds of hours of combat and experienced all the highs and lows that you would expect from those experiences. But I'm proud to have been a part of such a profound event that honored a former President and fellow combat Veteran. I would welcome the opportunity to do it all again.

CPT Kevin Counts

"...TOO LATE SIR...ALL TH' WARRANT PILOTS ARE FLYING, I CAN GIVE
YOU TWO POSTCARD DIRECT-COMMISSION FINANCE GUYS..."

ODIN 6

In 2012, the Army deployed me to Afghanistan as the commander of Task Force Observe, Detect, Identify, and Neutralize (TF ODIN-AFG). TF ODIN was a new concept to collect, synthesize and transmit to combat units very specific intelligence using state of the art intelligence technologies integrated into commercial aircraft. The unit was self-contained with everything needed to get intelligence as rapidly as possible to any unit on the battlefield. TF ODIN supported US and coalition forces across the entire country. On the surface, it looked like a flying circus with an assortment of different aircraft but as a battlefield tool, it was rapidly becoming the "go to capability," as the higher ups like to call it. And as the commander of the organization my call sign was ODIN 6.

This was not my first combat deployment. I had two earlier deployments to Iraq, but this was my first deployment to Afghanistan. Flying in Iraq had its own challenges and in no way prepared me for the weather and terrain in Afghanistan which was entirely in a league of its own. The country had little to no weather reporting stations, rapidly changing conditions of wind, dust, visibility and turbulence to mention only a few. The closest I'd come in my career to this type of flying environment was an assignment to Fort Carson, Colorado in the late 90s as a helicopter pilot. However, even the analogy to Colorado is probably a poor one in that the terrain and weather are exponentially worse in Afghanistan, not to mention, we had a determined enemy trying to shoot us down.

Like most areas in that part of the world, the summer months are usually dry and dusty. Afghanistan was no different. The dry and dusty conditions combine with winds that swept down the mountains creating, "pop-up" dust storms and other unpredictable weather. We did our best to account for all this unpredictability during our in-depth flight planning, but no amount of planning ever seemed to capture all the challenges. As luck would have it, our rotation was in May, just in time for the dry season and dust storms.

Approach lights during a sandstorm at the airfield in Afghanistan

For most military pilots who've been in the business long enough, it's nothing we haven't dealt with before. But the 20,000 plus foot mountain peaks in Afghanistan made it a little more high adventure than most other areas of the world. Weather forecasting in this land locked country was more art than science. The old joke that weather forecasters are the only profession that can be wrong more than they're right and still keep a job was an often-used comment at the airfield. That isn't a slam against the tremendous meteorological support we received from the Air Force. It was just another of the many challenges and pressures faced in an environment that was trying to kill us at every possible turn.

At TF ODIN, we flew highly modified commercial airplanes. One version was the venerable and versatile Beech King Air, or C-12 to use the military nomenclature. The TF ODIN fleet had been improved with the latest enhanced weather and terrain avoidance technology. Those improvements aided in our situational awareness and decision-making to avoid encountering potentially hazardous weather conditions. Few military aircraft were equipped with the technology provided to TF ODIN airplanes and we greatly appreciated it. Some of us "old timers" would reminisce and make remarks about how different it would be operating over here with some of the Vietnam era avionics we were using up until 9/11 and our current war time operations. We also developed a respect for the Soviet pilots that operated over here in the 80s.

We'd had a good run of weather through most of July and I was on the schedule for a night mission. Flying at night adds an additional complexity to an already high-risk mission. The only advantage was it made it harder for the enemy to target us.

We went through our usual pre-flight routine and mission briefing. That night we were doing what we considered a more mundane mission, so even with all the dangers and risks of our environment, we looked at these as less stressful missions. If the weather cooperated, night flying could be quite beautiful with the stars and clarity at our altitude. I was looking forward to the escape the cockpit provided me and the time away from phones, email, and all the other things that normally occupied my days. For an Army Aviation commander, the airplane is a sanctuary. The airplane is a retreat from the pressures of command. A quiet and enjoyable place that allowed me to do the one thing that made all the other aspects of my profession as an officer bearable, fly. For the true pilot, nothing beats being in the air. The sanctuary, my retreat was calling me and I was ready to go.

The weather was looking good for the duration of the mission but our meteorological team was forecasting low visibility due to seasonal sand storms about two hours after our expected arrival time back at home base. Also, Army regulations are similar to the FAA's regulations for alternates and fuel reserves, so we were carrying our regulation fuel reserve for the night flight. Surprisingly, the weather forecast was so good, that we weren't required to file for an alternate airfield. As a result of the forecast and the fact that we didn't need an alternate, we planned for additional time over the target that night. However, experience and prudence mandated that we would still check the weather at alternate airfields in case our home base couldn't accommodate our arrival due to an attack or other non-weather event that could cause a runway closure.

Depending on what was going on over the target area, we would sometimes leave early for home to give us enough fuel to get to an alternate and then some. But combat could cause things to change rapidly on the ground and our enemy was adapt at creating chaos at the most inopportune time. Ironically, everything that could go wrong for us that night did and as an adventure in flying, I hope to never have it go so wrong ever again.

After completing our mission briefing and pre-flight we strapped into the aircraft. We were a small crew for this mission with two pilots and an Aerial Sensor Operator (ASO) to operate the sensor equipment. The ASOs were the true unsung heroes and gave 100% on every mission. Many a Soldier on the ground owes their life to these ASOs, yet few will ever realize it.

We had the ability to adjust crew members based on mission and training needs. In a small twin turboprop, the crew size also resulted in a tradeoff for fuel, something we never thought we had enough of. Thankfully this night it was only three of us. Looking back on it, the extra weight of an additional crew member and their gear could have made for a very different outcome including a dead crew and destroyed aircraft.

View over the Hindu Kush from an earlier and less eventful mission

Blissfully unaware of what was in store for us, we took off. The climb out was uneventful and we were cleared into the flight levels to get up over the infamous Hindu Kush mountain range. As we had hoped and had been briefed, we had a full moon and starry night helping us out. While the sky was not totally clear, we had high clouds above us but unlimited visibility at our altitude. Even this time of year the highest peaks of the mountains shined with the moonlit snow on them. With the moon light reflecting off the snow-covered peaks, the glow of the aircraft instruments and purr of the Pratt and Whitney turbine engines setting the mood, we were in a beautiful yet surreal environment reminiscent of the night time scenes in the movie Avatar, or the glow of those psychedelic black light posters. The night was so beautiful and calming, not to mention the time of night it was, it was easy to slip into a false sense of security. We relied on routine, discipline and experience to remain vigilant. We were a well-seasoned crew and even though we appreciated the serenity we knew it could go to hell in a handbasket before we knew what hit us.

Getting close to our target area and having cleared some of the more significant terrain, we started a descent to our mission altitude; which, put us significantly lower than the surrounding mountainous terrain. Sightseeing and serenity were over, it was all business now. The terrain also meant that we were not in radar contact: Night VFR, as the FAA would call it. The terrain awareness and weather technology were now earning its keep by doing what radar would have done for us if available. It was also important to maintaining absolute situational awareness of the terrain around so as to not become a "controlled flight into terrain" statistic. Again, I go back to my earlier comment about learning to fly in airplanes with 1960s technology and the appreciation of modern terrain avoidance "magic boxes."

In the cockpit, we spent a couple hours "boring holes" in the night sky as we were fond of saying and running out of stories while in the back, the ASO was busy with the mission at hand.

In the mist of our pilot boredom, the ASO called up front over the intercom to see how much fuel we had left. Even though it wasn't unusual for the ASO to check in with us up front, by the excitement in his voice, I knew that our boredom was over. We told the ASO we could give him another hour on station but that would cut into any possibility of landing anywhere but home base. Given our weather briefing and what we were seeing with our own eyes, the offer to stay on station made sense and still provided for our legal reserves. "Standby," was his only response. A few minutes later, the ASO requested we stay the extra hour. He was busy, so I didn't ask what was going on. Lives were now at stake on the ground, that much I was sure of.

The ASO had direct communication with the ground forces and because of our equipment, we could provide support for and coordinate with other ground forces if and when necessary or requested. We were about thirty minutes into our "extension" when the ASO told us that our routine mission had turned into a full-blown high priority troops-in-contact, or TIC as we called them. Because of the nature of a TIC, it was the highest priority situation we would ever support. As a result, most of the rules were thrown out the window. We were in combat so would stay as long as our nerve allowed and risk landing on fumes or be prepared to pull a Doolittle Raiders Part II, without parachutes in our case.

Now that we understood the ground situation, we got busy up front working out contingencies. Kenny Loggins' Danger Zone (The theme to the movie Top Gun) was nowhere in the background when the mighty C-12 was on the job – it was more like the Tippi Turtle theme song I would sing to my kids. The balance of staying too long or breaking station too early tonight now had life and death consequences. Although we didn't need an alternate, we were sacrificing any additional fuel reserves we had so that we would only have enough for one or maybe two approaches (theoretically). For me, this was a little unnerving, particularly in this part of the world where Murphy's Law was more of the rule and less of the exception. And, as a commander, whatever example I set in the aircraft would be the standard all the pilots would adhere to. We needed to provide support, but could not afford to be too much of a "cowboy." To make the stakes even higher, our relief aircraft had been delayed due to a maintenance issue. Once we left, the troops on the ground would be without support unless we could coordinate for another aircraft to be launched or diverted to our location, and soon.

As the TIC continued, our fuel situation grew more and more critical. We needed enough fuel to climb back over the mountains and then could try and conserve some fuel by requesting minimum vectoring and a continuous descent to landing. I recall briefing my copilot with a somewhat fatalistic attitude and smirk: "We're going to land somewhere in Afghanistan with, or without, the engines running."

As we're trying to get a status on the TIC from the ASO, we received the worse possible news we wanted to hear: Weather conditions at our home base were deteriorating rapidly. Apparently, nobody informed the sandstorm that it could not arrive before our scheduled landing time. According to our fuel computer, we would be able to make one, maybe two approaches. The night was not so serene anymore.

With the sandstorm approaching the only airfield we knew we had the gas to land at and earlier than forecast, Murphy did throw us a bone. A sister Service airplane with similar capabilities contacted us that they could and would be at our location shortly to relieve us and to handle the TIC. Even though we would still have our own challenges, we were relieved that we would not be leaving the ground unit in combat without support. Once the other airplane was on station, we pointed the nose toward home and began a climb to get over the mountains.

As I was trying to perform feats of alchemy by climbing with minimum fuel burn the copilot was doing what we call running fuel burns using his brain, a stubby pencil, and a piece of paper. It's not that we didn't trust the fancy fuel management computer embedded in the aircraft's Flight Management System (FMS), we old timers who started our Army aviation careers in the venerable UH-1H Huey helicopter trusted our Vietnam veteran instructor pilots and their skills of computing fuel calculations with pencil and paper more than the FMS. As the copilot completed his calculations, the good news was we had enough fuel to make it. The bad news was we weren't going to have enough fuel to divert anywhere else from our position high over the Hindu Kush mountain range. Descending at idle to conserve gas, I was trying to formulate the explanation I was going to give to my higher headquarters commander on why he was short one intel asset, assuming we survived an off airport landing. Fifteen minutes out from home base, we made our initial contact with the tower on the radio and it wasn't good news.

Tower was reporting zero visibility, high winds and a sandstorm. To add a cherry on top of our sundae, the airfield had been under a rocket attack prior to the arrival of the sandstorm. An Explosive Ordnance Detachment (EOD) team was still inspecting the runway for damage and looking for any unexploded ordinance. Unexploded ordinance has a tendency to become "exploded ordinance" when you run over it. Tower politely informed us that they were currently diverting aircraft to alternate airfields and asked us to do the same. We responded back in a less polite and less calm manner that we were low on fuel and would "assume risk" for the approach and landing. This "assume risk" phrase is a phrase that Army pilots sometimes throw out as sort of a legal out for the controller in case you, the pilot, ball it up.

The controller came back and said he was unable to clear us for the approach or to land and that the instrument approach system and the runway landing lights were shut down to reduce the risk to the EOD team which was still out inspecting the runway and taxiways. The controller told us we either needed to hold or divert immediately. The controller also felt compelled to also explained to me that the weather was below approach minimums and by regulation I was not authorized to try the approach and landing. While this is true according to

Air Force regulations, in the Army (on occasion the Army does get it right) we're allowed to "attempt" the approach even though the current weather is below minimums. As I'm explaining Army regulations to the Air Force controller, I was burning precious fuel and my patience was starting to rapidly run out.

With the stress, adrenaline and frustration of the evening, I blew up. I explained in terms and verbiage, that would make a Sailor proud, that we were going to shoot the approach and land and that I and the law of gravity didn't give a damn about Air Force regulations or unexploded ordinance. I then declared an emergency and told him to get the Tower Chief on the radio ASAP. While I'm going off on the controller, my copilot was tuning up the instrument approach frequencies and getting everything else set up all the while giving me the bad news on our fuel situation: "We're on fumes." After what seemed like an eternity, the tower chief came up on the radio and said the airfield instruments were back on and we should start picking up the signal. We were cleared for the approach "at our own risk." The Tower Chief also let us know that the EOD team had cleared the runway. I don't know if this was an attempt at humor on the part of the Tower Chief or EOD team, but the EOD team requested we tell the Tower Chief if we "run across any ordinance on landing." I felt like replying that if they saw or heard an explosion that we found something, but instead I remained silent and elicited an odd and out of place chuckle to myself.

With the equipment back on, we picked up the runway directional signal and turned inbound on final. The aircraft was being buffeted by very strong winds that were driving the sandstorm. With only minutes to land or run out of gas, the Tower Chief called us with some additional bad news that they couldn't get the runway lights to come on and had a team out working on it and visibility was still "zero-zero". We were all getting anxious as we were only minutes out from touchdown.

Even though we had a directional beacon the copilot announced we weren't picking up the glide-slope and reminded me that we only had enough fuel for one approach and landing. No pressure.

I told tower about the glide-slope and he said he didn't know what the issue with the glide-slope was. Now, instead of being able to go as low as 200 feet above the ground, I would be flying blind once I was 400 feet above the ground. Even though we were going to land one way or the other, the ability to follow a radio beam that additional 200 feet down was a big deal tonight. Thank you, Murphy, for giving me a full plate tonight.

The Tower Chief re-cleared, again at our own risk, for the localizer approach. I continued my descent, pulled the power back and strained to locate the runway somewhere in the sand and wind-swept blackness before us. 600 feet was nothing but darkness and silence. At 400 feet the copilot saw very dim lights which in his terror, mistook for apron lights. Moments later, around 300 feet his terror turned into absolute joy when he shouted out "runway lights in sight." At 200 feet, I looked up to the happiest sight I have ever seen in my flying career, we were lined up dead center with the runway. As the wheels touched down, I exhaled deeply. It actually ended up being one of my better landings. I told tower we were on the ground as they still could not see us due to the visibility.

Last flight as ODIN 6 and as an Army aviator – April 2nd, 2013.

As we slowed the aircraft to make the taxiway into parking, we were all elated and laughing with relief until the ASO mentioned the unexploded ordinance and possible taxiway damage. As if he and the Tower Chief were tag teaming the point, the Tower Chief cleared us into parking, again, at our own risk. We ceased the pre-celebration and cautiously made our way to the parking ramp keeping an eye out for taxiway damage and unexploded ordinance. Now on the ground, we made some bad jokes about it being just our luck to survive all of that to run over some unexploded ordinance as we taxied to the parking apron. Thankfully it was just that, a bad joke to end the night. We parked and shut down without further incident.

I've never smoked in my life with the exception of an occasional cigar but after we closed out the aircraft logbook and our other ritualistic post-flight activities, I noticed the ASO over in a smoking area just off of the flight line having a cigarette. I walked over and without even saying a word he handed me one and lit it up for me with shaky hands. I realized at that moment his weren't the only hands shaking.

By then, night was becoming morning and it was time to give the wife a call as it was evening back in the US. We had a nice chat about nothing noteworthy. And while I loved calling home and dearly missed my family, there are just things you can't explain or expect another person, even a family member or close friend, to understand. This night was one of them. I don't think there are words that capture all the emotions that go into an event like this night. It brings true meaning to an old cliché: You just had to be there.

LTC Kevin Counts

THE GCA CONTROLLER....

"...ARMY 552... APPROACHING GLIDESCOPE... ON COURSE... WHEELS SHOULD BE DOWN..."

"ON GLIDESCOPE... DESCEND TO ONE-THOUSAND FEET... TURN RIGHT HEADING ONE-SIX-NINE"

"...GOING BELOW GLIDESCOPE... TURN FURTHER RIGHT HEADING ONE-SEVEN-FOUR..."

"...STOP DESCENT... STOP TURN... ARMY 552... SPEAK TO ME... OVER..."

"... GCA THIS IS ARMY 552 WE LANDED FIVE MINUTES AGO... CO PILOT FORGOT TO TELL YOU... SORRY 'BOUT THAT..."

CONTRIBUTORS*

Army 427	Craig Randall
Army 089	Craig Randall
Army 261	Craig Randall
Boss 88	Craig Randall
Black 5	Craig Randall
Cyclops 41	CPT AB
Nail 18	Steve Koenig
Castor 07	Steve Koenig
Hawk 30	Steve Koenig
Vigilant 6	Steve Koenig
Aloma 6	Steve Koenig
Army 58CL	Randy Cupit
Grizzly 22	Steve Koenig
Golden Knight 608	Kevin Counts
ODIN 6	Kevin Counts

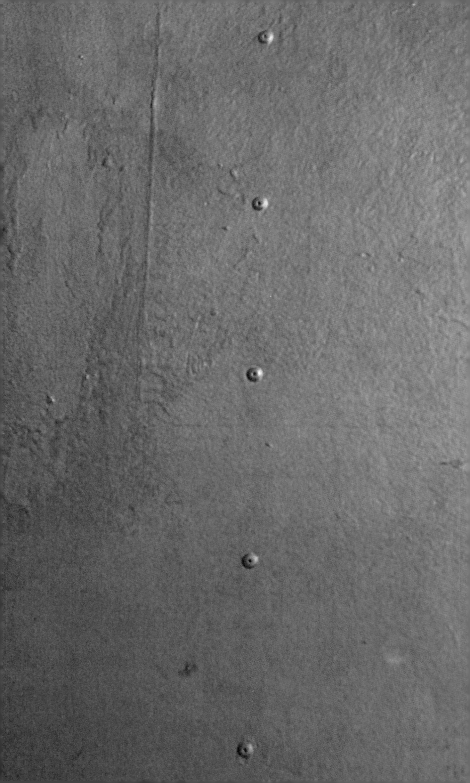

BIOGRAPHIES

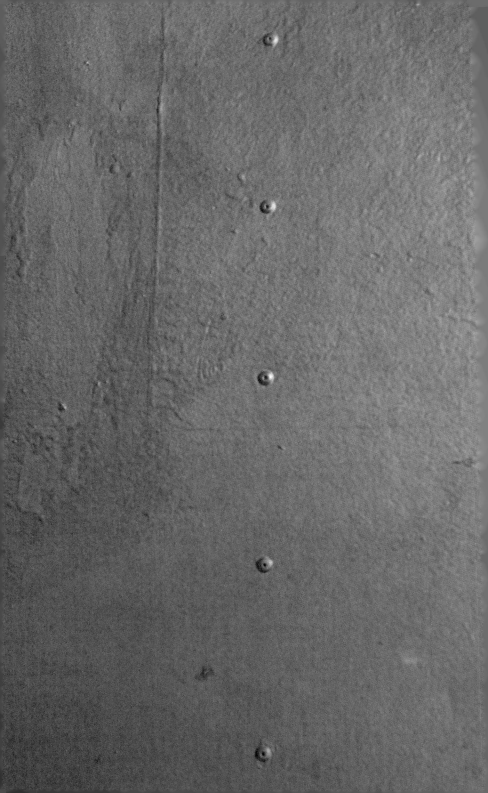

CRAIG V. RANDALL

hief Warrant Officer 4 (CW4) Craig V. Randall, US Army (Retired), enlisted in the US Army in 1972 and was the Distinguished Graduate from flight school at Fort Rucker in 1974. Notable flying assignments included: "Hard Core 36," the 227th Aviation Battalion, 1st Cavalry Division, Fort Hood Texas, flying OH-58A/C Kiowa scout helicopters and was pilot and Aide de Campe for General Jack N. Merritt; the US Army Field Artillery Center Flight Detachment, Fort Sill, Oklahoma; the Presidio, San Francisco, California; 4th Squadron, 7th Cavalry of the 2nd Infantry Division, South Korea as "Mad Dog 33," flying AH-1 Cobra helicopters and OH-58A/C Kiowa with duties as the Air Liaison Officer to the 3rd ROK Infantry Regiment on the DMZ; 6th Army Fixed Wing Standardization Officer, the Presidio; flying SH-3G Sea King helicopters to and from the USS Coral Sea to validate Army helicopter operations from naval vessels; V Corps and Europe

Fixed Wing Standardization Officer in Frankfurt, Germany with duties as C-12 "Huron" VIP pilot for General Colin Powell, General George Joulwan, and Lieutenant General John Woodmansee; VIP pilot for General Frederic Franks, 7th Corps for Operation Desert Shield; US Army South Standardization Officer with duty in the Panama Canal Zone and Howard Air Force Base flying missions throughout the Americas. In 1992 Craig joined the US Army Intelligence and Security Command at Fort Meade, Maryland where he served in a classified flight position supporting the National Security Agency until his retirement in 1994.

Craig's s awards and decorations include the Legion of Merit, Humanitarian Service Medal, Korea Defense Service Medal, Southwest Asia Service Medal, the American Honor Spirit Medal and various unit and service citations. He is a graduate of the Warrant Officer Senior Course.

After retirement, Craig worked as Chief Pilot, Jet International Management, an international helicopter and jet flight company flying Falcon 50 and 900 jets, Augusta Helicopters, and B200 King Airs turboprops. Notable clients included Prime Minister Margaret Thatcher. In 1997, Craig formed Cascade Air Inc. an aerospace consulting firm with numerous Fortune 500 clients including: Dassault Falcon Jet, British Petroleum, HBO, and Black and Decker. He also served as Director, Managing Partner, and CEO of Pacific Jets Corporation in California, an aircraft company that sold the Dassault jet. In 2003, Craig moved to London as managing partner for Data Storage Limited (an intelligence and security firm) and The Rexford Penn Group, a publishing group. He later joined FlightSafety International as a Program Manager of training operations for airline operations, military liaison and Citation 560XLS jet training. Craig has logged over 13,880 hours in more than 25 types of civilian and military airplanes and helicopters. His worldwide adventures include 76 Trans-Atlantic crossings as Captain and circumnavigating the globe three times. He is currently working on a DC-3 rating.

His aviation art is displayed in private and public collections worldwide and he is the winner of the Army Art Contest, EAA Art Competition, National Air and Space Museum Art Competition, and the Museum of Naval Aviation Art Competition. Additionally, he is an accomplished musician and motorcyclist.

Craig is a life member of: The American Society of Aviation Artists, Association of the United States Army and the Air Force Association, The Army Aviation Association of America, VFW, DAV, and the American Motorcyclist Association.

Born in Berkeley, California, Craig now lives on an ancestral family ranch in the mountains of Oregon.

Craig's company on the cover of Professional Pilot Magazine

The Hunter Becomes the Hunted, 1987

Craig's art on the cover   One of Craig's clients, Margret Thatcher,
of Aviation Digest 1980   former Prime Minister of England

KEVIN E. COUNTS

olonel Kevin Counts enlisted in the Army in 1987 as an Infantryman. After completion of his enlistment, he attended Radford University in Radford, Virginia on an Army ROTC Scholarship and received a Bachelor of Science degree in Criminal Justice. He was commissioned a Second Lieutenant in the Aviation Branch in 1994.

His assignments included Aviation Platoon Leader, Assistant Squadron S2 and Regimental S1, 3rd Armored Cavalry Regiment, Ft Carson, Colorado, (1995 to 1998); S1 and S3 Plans Officer, 3rd Military Intelligence Battalion (Aerial Exploitation), Cp Humphreys, Korea, (1999 to 2000) and A Company Commander (ARL), (2000 to 2002); Aviation Detachment Commander, United States Army Parachute Team 'The Golden Knights', Fort Bragg, North Carolina (2002 to 2006); S3, 15th Military Intelligence Battalion (Aerial Exploitation), Ft Hood, Texas (2007 to 2010) including two Operation Iraqi Freedom deployments; Headquarters, Department of the Army G2, Airborne ISR Officer in the Operations and Plans Directorate (2010-2012); Commander, 306th Military Intelligence Battalion (Aerial Exploitation) and Task Force ODIN-AFG, Operation Enduring Freedom (2012 to 2013) Afghanistan; ISR Test Division Chief, Operational Test Command, at Ft Hood, Texas (2013 to 2015). United States Forces Korea (USFK) J2 Chief of ISR Operations (2015-2016); and USFK J2 Director of Intelligence Operations (2016-2018). Colonel Counts retired in 2019.

Colonel Counts' military education includes the Aviation Officer Basic Course, Military Intelligence Officer Advance Course, Fixed-Wing Multi-Engine Qualification Course, and the Command and General Staff Course. He is qualified in multiple fixed and rotary wing aircraft. In 2007 he received a Master of Science degree in Business Administration from Central Michigan University.

His decorations and badges include the Bronze Star Medal, Meritorious Service Medal (4th Oak Leaf Cluster), Air Medal (Second Award), Army Commendation Medal (1st Oak Leaf Cluster), Army Achievement Medal (2nd Oak Leaf Cluster), Army Staff Identification Badge, and the Master Army Aviator Badge with over 4,000 flight hours.

Kevin now flies for a defense contractor in various locations around the world.

Colonel Counts is the son of Gene and Judy Counts of Haysi, Virginia. He resides with his wife Jean in San Antonio, TX. Their daughter Sarah resides in Rochester, New York and son James resides in New Britain, Connecticut.

Personal Note from Kevin:

"I want to give credit to the professional aviators, parachutists, support personnel, and leadership I served with during the four years I was privileged to wear the black and gold of the Golden Knights. I am humbled to this day to have served with them and time will never diminish the respect I have for my former teammates. I treasure the time we spent together."

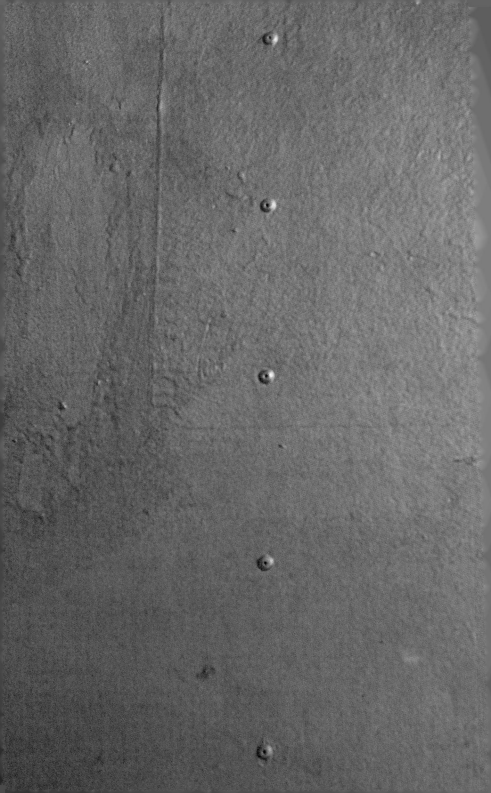

G. ROBERT (BOB) SNEAD

C W4 Bob Snead enlisted in the Army in 1952 and participated in both the Dominican Republic invasion and multiple tours of Vietnam. He completed Warrant Officer Candidate School at Ft Wolters, TX in 1969. A veteran of 30 years of military service as a decorated dual-rated pilot, Bob earned 41 Air Medals, three Purple Hearts, three Vietnam Crosses of Gallantry with Silver Stars, two Bronze Stars with V Devices, the Combat Infantry Badge, Senior Parachutist's Badge, and the Master Aviator Badge with over four thousand flight hours. He was awarded the Army Aviation Association of America Bronze Order of St. Michael in 2006.

During his military career his cartoons drew praise and problems, raves and rages. Yet, with all the challenges he refused to change his subject matter . . . everyday military life.

Bob captured military life in a style that he considers "closer to" (Bill) Mauldin than anybody. Sort of the 80's "Willie and Joe." Like Mauldin, Snead often encountered official resistance to some of his cartoons. But his popularity was such that the Army Times published his cartoons for more than twenty years. His works have also appeared in a variety of military post publications in the United States and overseas, as well as in many civilian publications culminating in his book of cartoons entitled: "Hours of Boredom."

Bob's interest in art and cartooning began in elementary school in Charlotte, North Carolina and has not stopped with his retirement from the United States Army in 1982. His art has been exhibited in Europe, Africa, Central America, and at major shows and galleries in the United States.

Bob's determination to succeed led him to study at the Chouinard Art Institute in Los Angeles, California, the University of Mainz in Mainz, Germany, under the tutelage of the late O.A Williams of Charlotte, North Carolina and Dr. Wolfgang Braun of West Germany. He also studied under the noted impressionist Salviano Constantin.

In addition to his accomplishments as a cartoonist and artist, Bob has taken his story of the "Buffalo Soldiers" to the stage. As an actor he brings to life in an unusual one-act play: "The Life and Times of Lt. Henry Ossian Flipper," the first black graduate of the United States Military Academy (West Point.) Snead has researched Flipper and the legendary Buffalo Soldiers for more than 50 years and has also performed 'Held in Trust,' written by Bea Bragg and Richard Hobbs, for more than a quarter-century.

Bob Snead as Lt. Henry Ossian Flipper

Bob's paintings hang in the Texas Governor's Mansion as well as around the world. He was appointed Artist-In-Residence for the University of Texas, El Paso African American Studies in 1998.

"The Errand of Corporal Ross," painted by Snead was selected as the model for the Buffalo Soldier Memorial erected at Fort Bliss in 1998.

"The Errand of Corporal Ross," painted by Bob Snead, model for the
Buffalo Soldier Memorial erected at Fort Bliss in 1998.

On November 5, 1999, Bob was inducted into the El Paso International Hall of Fame for Visual Arts. Bob was selected to represent El Paso on the Texas Commission on the Arts and was also a Bush-appointee to the commission that selected the Texas design on the U.S. Mint's state quarters. He received the Star on the Mountain Award from the City of El Paso in April 2016 and the Buffalo Soldiers Educational and Historical Committee award from Kansas City.

Buffalo Soldiers Educational and Historical Committee award from Kansas City

Most recently, Bob donated 11 of his prized Buffalo Solider paintings to the Armed Services YMCA Lodge of El Paso valued at over $10,000.

Armed Services YMCA Lodge of El Paso

RANDY E. CUPIT

C W4(Ret) Randy Cupit is a Master Aviator who enlisted in the Army in 1980 and spent 26 years serving in the US Army flying UH60/EH-60/S-70/UH-1 helicopters and Army modified B200 /B300/ DHC-7 ISR aircraft. During his career he served as Contracting Officer Representative, production Control Officer, Maintenance Officer, and Test Pilot in assignments throughout the world.

He has a bachelor's degree from Embry-Riddle Aeronautical University and is a graduate of numerous Army flight and Warrant officer schools.

In retirement he is a program manager and government SP/IP/ ME/MP for fixed wing aircraft for a defense contractor supporting military operations around the world. He has an FAA Airline Transport Pilot, Airplane; Commercial Pilot, Helicopter; Multi-Engine Instructor, and Certified Instrument Flight Instructor.

STEVEN T KOENIG

C olonel (retired) Steve Koenig was commissioned an Army Aviator through ROTC at Xavier University in 1986. He held leadership positions from Platoon Leader through Battalion Commander and had assignments in Germany, Korea, Colombia (South America), Ft Hood, Ft Bliss, West Point, the Pentagon and Iraq. He is qualified in two types of Army helicopters and five different Army airplanes. He was in the Pentagon on September 11, 2001 and served in different rolls while deployed to Iraq for various lengths of time in 2004, 2005 and 2006. In his role as Senior Aviation Officer to the Army G-2, he handled 23 separate military intelligence aviation programs with a total budget of $1.23 billion dollars. He was directly responsible for the development, organization, equipping and deployment of Task

Force ODIN – Afghanistan; Army MARSS (AFG), TACOPS and VADER aircraft development and deployment. He also wrote classified doctrine, tactics, techniques and procedures for Intelligence, Surveillance, and Reconnaissance aircraft employment in asymmetric operations. He is a graduate of numerous Army schools including Aviation Officer Basic Course, Military Intelligence Advance Course and The Command and General Staff College. He has a Bachelor of Science degree in Industrial Relations from Xavier University and a Master of Science in Education and Leadership from Long Island University. He retired after 24 years and his awards and decorations include Master Aviator with over 4000 flight hours, the Army Parachutist Badge, the Legion of Merit, the Iraq Campaign Medal with one battle star and many other awards.

He is a life member of both the Army Aviation Association of America and the VFW, and a member of the American Legion, AUSA and the Disable American Veterans. He is a recipient of the Army Aviation Association of America Order of St Michael (Bronze) and the Military Intelligence Corps Association Knowlton Award.

In retirement, he worked in Business Development for both King Aerospace, INC and Commuter Air Technology. He is an avid General Aviation airplane owner and pilot owning two Rockwell Commander 112TCs and an ex-RAF primary trainer, a Scottish Aviation Bulldog. He is presently employed as a commercial Boeing 777 airline pilot. He holds FAA type ratings in the EMB-145, ERJ 170/175/190 and B777.

He has been recognized by both La Salle High School, Cincinnati, Ohio (Community Pillar Award 2012) and Xavier University, Cincinnati, Ohio (ROTC Hall of Fame 2017) for his contributions.

He is a volunteer with the Knights of Columbus, on the La Salle High School Veterans Appreciation Board, the XU ROTC Alumni Advisory Board and a member of the Civil Air Patrol.

In 2018, he established Brajer Animo, LLC.

He is married to LTC (retired) Cindy Koenig for 32 blessed years and they reside outside of Columbus Ohio.

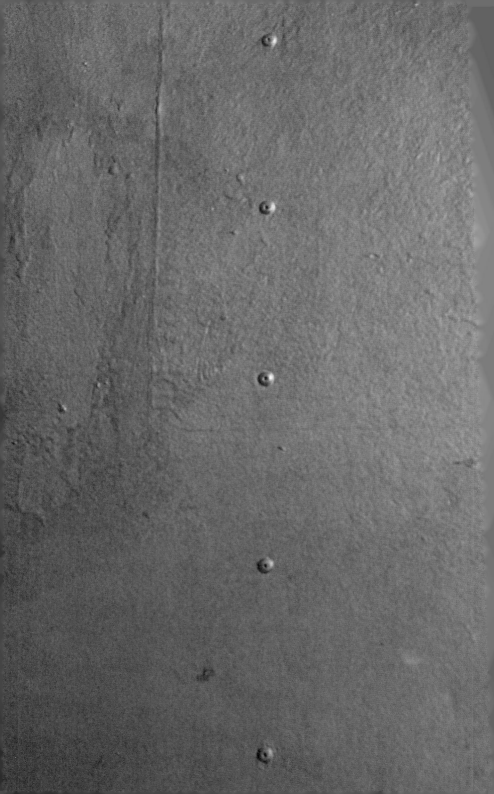

SEPTEMBER 11, 2001

O n September 11, 2001, my wife, Cindy, and I (both Majors) were at our offices in the Pentagon. Cindy was working in the AOC–Army Operations Center (Army Staff) and I was working in the NMCC–National Military Command Center (JCS–Joint Chief of Staff). Like the rest of the world, we were both watching the news from New York City that morning and starting another day as "Staff Officers" in the highest headquarters of the US military.

The Pentagon: Pre-9-11-01

National Military Command Center (NMCC) 2D921

Army Operations Center (Basement, Corridor 7)

Aircraft point of impact (approximate)

When the airplane struck the Pentagon – before it made the news – Cindy telephoned and asked if I heard the explosion on her side of the building. Now most people don't realize this, but the Pentagon is one of the largest enclosed office buildings in the world, home to over 25,000 employees in its offices, shops and corridors. As many as another 25,000 people – tourist, dignitaries, military and political representatives – visit the building daily. I've been told that if you stood it up like a skyscraper it would almost be as tall as the Empire State Building, in New York City. So, when you think of an airplane hitting the Pentagon, what you experienced that day was different depending on your location within.

My office was as far away and in the most secure location in the entire building from the impact point as possible. In response to Cindy's question, I told her no; that we were watching the developments in NYC. She told me in a calm and professional but slightly tense voice that something definitely exploded on her side of the building, an evacuation order had been given for the entire Army Staff with the exception of the AOC, and that smoke was coming into the AOC thru the ventilation system. Lastly, she asked me to call her parents and recommended I call mine to let them know that we were okay before it became national news.

Within minutes of the attack, military decision making was already reorienting priorities. The Services were as standing up CATs – Crisis Action Team – protocols (A process which streamlines many procedures during a national crisis.)

I told Cindy I loved her, hung up, and went into my boss's office to ask if he had heard anything about an explosion somewhere in the building. I told him what Cindy had told me and as she requested, went back to my cubical and called our parents to let them know that we were both okay. Even before my boss returned to our office, the news began reporting the attack on the Pentagon.

In a certain sense, time seemed to move much quicker and of course, there was a bit of chaos happening simultaneously. The news announced the attack, the NMCC was told to evacuate the building. Certain war time protocols were enacted as well. As a result of the decisions and orders coming out, I would not hear from (except an email) or see Cindy for almost four days.

Evacuating the Pentagon was like doing fire drill practice. My organization exited the building by an entrance near the Potomac River and security directed us to move towards the marina near the river. Looking back at the building, black billowing smoke could be seen on the far side and the secondary explosions caused by the initial attack could be heard. There was a slight smell of fuel, but not overpowering as we were well away from our "ground zero." From far away, all of us standing by the marina probably looked like a group assembling for an outdoor concert. We were standing around, discussing "what if" scenarios, trying to make cell calls and a few even took some selfies. Mostly we were left feeling helpless, wondering what would happen next. Oddly, commercial airliners were still flying down the Potomac on visual approach to Regan National Airport just a few miles away.

As we milled around, leadership was trying to account for personnel and deciding what to do with non-essential employees (let them go home or say in the area…just in case). It was at this point that the cell phone networks overloaded and nobody could call anybody. (I was really glad I got a call out to our families before we evacuated.) A small group of my department were told to make our way to an off-site location know as "The Rock." From there we would set up our CAT and spend the remainder of the day and night away from D.C.

Before hitting the road for the Rock, while sitting outside on the grass, just watching the black billowing smoke and feeling completely helpless, an Air Force F-16 Falcon made a very low pass over the Potomac River as if performing at an air show. A tremendous roar went up from all of us "spectators" as he climbed into the blue, sunny sky, after burner roaring. I remember thinking to myself: "GO GET'EM!" And then, as I thought about my guttural reaction, I laughed. My co-workers asked me why I was laughing, so I told them. "How ironic to cheer for an unarmed fighter seeking vengeance against an unidentified attacker who is probable continents away." But I will never forget the morale boost that fly-by gave me and all of us that morning, and I knew that WE would have our vengeance.

Since the roads were jammed pack with the entire government sending home all employees, the drive to the Rock took much longer than normal. The access road had both military and law enforcement personnel in full battle gear manning check points which caused even more delays in getting into the site. We arrived after the Twin Towers had collapsed and unlike war game exercises, we were a focused, motivated and dare I say, a blood thirsty group – Somebody attacked our country….. Somebody killed our citizens…… Somebody was cowardly……. Somebody was going to pay………

CAT operations that night purposed may response options. Some were rejected and some were incorporated into what has historically become known as Operation Enduring Freedom and Operation Iraqi Freedom.

Suffice it to say that the next several weeks were very chaotic for the both Cindy and I. We became 12-hour shift workers preparing for a new war. The Pentagon smelt of fire and smoke for weeks after the attack.

The myriads of temporary tentage, numerous ambulances, police and specially security vehicles, the sight of Army Military Police guarding the Pentagon in full combat equipment 24/7 (with rules on the use of deadly force) and all the emotions associated with the attack will always be present in our minds, especially around the anniversary.

We are both proud of our service on that day and throughout our careers. While I have no special mementos of that day, The Director of the Army AOC on 9-11 was more cognoscente of the historical significance of the event. He had members of his staff collect fragments of the building and chiseled numbers into each piece. Upon his departure from the Army Staff to assume command of the 1st Calvary Division, he presented each of his "Day 1" CAT members with a numbered commendation letter and piece of the Pentagon. The number on the stone matches the number annotated on his letter of appreciation. It is an incredible piece of history and fitting tribute for those who served in combat on US soil on the very first day of the War on Terror, a war that continues to the present day, America's longest war.

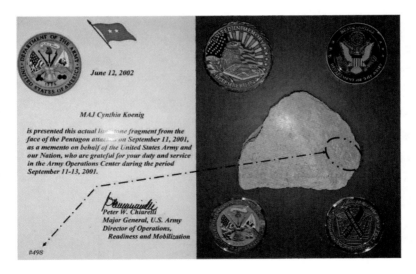

I hope the pictures add some worth to the words.......NEVER FORGET!

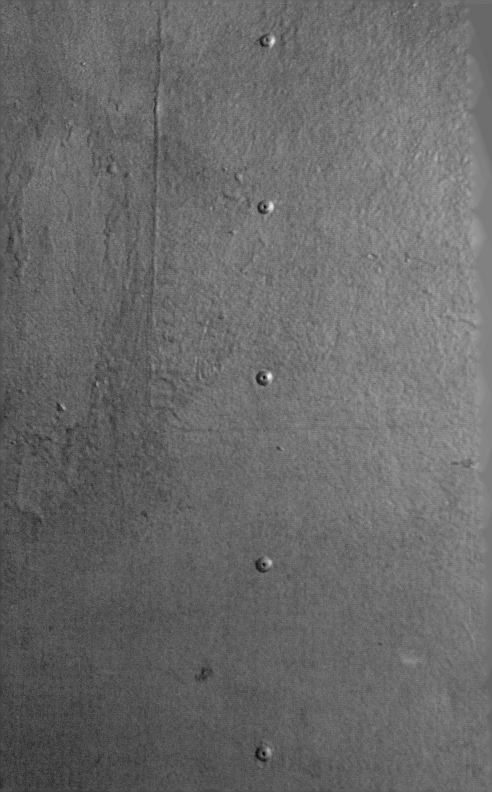

DEDICATION AND THANKS

C all Signs was inspired and is dedicated to the many Army fixed wing pilots who share stories and pictures on Face Book: US Army Fixed Wing page.

After making a comment that somebody should write some of this down, I took my own advice and began the two-year process of putting these stories together. Almost every picture was provided by the contributor of each story. All stories are original. Two stories were ghost written by a contributor who had firsthand knowledge of the events. All stories actually happened. I had hoped to have a few more stories as the Army flies a great number of diverse airplanes.

There are some great pictures that need voice and I am sure have some good "There I was" quality stories to go with them. Unfortunately, the owners of the pictures were not willing to participate in this book. It is interesting to note that:

1. The US Army has flown to North Korea supporting diplomatic efforts.

2. The Army used some very special powered gliders in Vietnam and in South America......

3. Metro Liners, B1900s have been used by the Army for VIP transport and logistic support for years.

4. Then there is the venerable C-23 Sherpa. The 100 knot wonder that hauls logistics all over and has been in operation since the

1980s. Sherpas supported combat operations in OIF. Flying an unpressurized low altitude turboprop is probably one of the most demanding jobs in the fix wing world.

5. Of course, there are places no one would ever volunteer to fly........

6. And airplanes that fought the cold war by just showing the colors in a walled city 119 miles inside a communist country (West Berlin which was in East Germany).

My thanks, love and prayers for the contributions and inspiration of Bob Snead. I was introduced to Bob Snead as a Lieutenant at Fort Rucker in 1986 when I bought a copy of *"Hours and Hours of Bordom...."*, his book of comics. His book has gone with me on every assignment throughout my career and it is safe to say that I lived many of his cartoons in one way or another.

In 2006 I met him for real by chance in El Paso, Texas. I walked into his framing store to get a picture framed. He was kind and unassuming and it took almost an hour to hear that he was both a retired Army Aviator and author of the cartoons that I enjoyed as a lieutenant. He was my guest of honor that fall at the unit formal and to this day my former Soldiers remember him and his entertaining comments. I was honored to present him with the Bronze Order of St. Michael, an honorary award from the Army Aviation Association of America in recognition for his aviation career.

I decided to ask for his participation with this book back in 2018. He was as generous and enthusiastic as the man I remember meeting in 2006. I will always cherish his humility, politeness and generosity.

Being able to republish his cartoons is value added to the endeavor to give something back to the community that I served and take so much pride in being a part of. The fact that his cartoons deal with Army fixed wing challenges in the 1960-70 and are still relevant today is a testament to Bob's understanding of the subject matter and that while the airplanes are the object, the human situations are the focus.

I can only hope and pray that Bob will share some of his Army aviation adventures in the future and that I can pay his kindness and generosity forward. Given his accomplishments both in uniform and as an artist, statesman and actor, he deserves to be inducted into the Army Aviation Hall of Fame. I hope that I can convince Quad A of that in the coming years.

Lastly, to my wife of 33 years who has had to listen to my flying stories for years and is happy that they will now be read by others (and that she won't have to listen to them anymore). Thank you for being my muse and biggest supporter. I hope we will have many more adventures in the years to come.